Empathy Book for Adults

CRAFTED BY SKRIUWER

Copyright © 2024 by Skriuwer.

All rights reserved. No part of this book may be used or reproduced in any form whatsoever without written permission except in the case of brief quotations in critical articles or reviews.

For more information, contact : **kontakt@skriuwer.com** (www.skriuwer.com)

TABLE OF CONTENTS

CHAPTER 1: WHAT IS EMPATHY?

- Definition of empathy as understanding and sharing another's feelings
- How empathy differs from sympathy and pity
- Why empathy is important in human connections
- The role of awareness, understanding, and response

CHAPTER 2: WHY EMPATHY MATTERS IN OUR DAILY LIVES

- Building stronger relationships through empathy
- Decreasing misunderstandings and conflicts
- Supporting emotional well-being
- Fostering kindness and community

CHAPTER 3: DIFFERENT KINDS OF EMPATHY

- Emotional empathy, cognitive empathy, and compassionate empathy
- Somatic empathy and its physical signs
- Balancing different empathy styles
- Culture and upbringing's impact on empathy

CHAPTER 4: BLOCKS TO EMPATHY AND HOW TO OVERCOME THEM

- Stress and overwhelm as empathy barriers
- Personal biases and fear of vulnerability
- Lack of time or attention in modern life
- Practical tips for breaking down empathy blocks

CHAPTER 5: THE ROLE OF BODY LANGUAGE IN EMPATHY

- *Recognizing common nonverbal cues*
- *Reading facial expressions and posture*
- *Using your own body language to show care*
- *Cultural differences in nonverbal communication*

CHAPTER 6: ACTIVE LISTENING TECHNIQUES

- *The difference between hearing and listening*
- *Key steps: focus, avoid interrupting, reflect, and validate*
- *Overcoming distractions and emotional reactions*
- *Building better communication and trust*

CHAPTER 7: EMPATHY IN ROMANTIC RELATIONSHIPS

- *Emotional closeness and trust through empathy*
- *Handling disagreements with understanding*
- *Supporting each other's growth and healing*
- *Overcoming common empathy challenges in love*

CHAPTER 8: EMPATHY IN THE WORKPLACE

- *Improved team communication and morale*
- *Leading with empathy to reduce turnover*
- *Resolving conflicts and building respect*
- *Practical ways to show care in professional settings*

CHAPTER 9: EMPATHY AND PARENTING

- *Why empathetic parenting matters for child development*
- *Using emotional vocabulary with kids*
- *Handling tantrums and discipline kindly*
- *Modeling empathy for children at different ages*

CHAPTER 10: CULTURAL DIFFERENCES AND EMPATHY

- Understanding the visible and invisible parts of culture
- Overcoming stereotypes and biases
- Building trust and respect across cultural lines
- Practical strategies for cross-cultural empathy

CHAPTER 11: DIGITAL COMMUNICATION AND EMPATHY

- Challenges of empathy in online spaces
- Practicing thoughtfulness on social media and messaging apps
- Dealing with online criticism or hostility calmly
- Building supportive digital communities

CHAPTER 12: BUILDING SELF-AWARENESS TO IMPROVE EMPATHY

- Connecting inner understanding with caring for others
- Spotting personal emotional triggers and biases
- Balancing empathy with self-care
- Daily habits for mindfulness and reflection

CHAPTER 13: HEALING EMOTIONAL WOUNDS THROUGH EMPATHY

- Types of emotional wounds and why they linger
- The role of empathy in validation and safe sharing
- Practicing self-empathy versus self-pity
- Empathy-based therapy and group support

CHAPTER 14: SETTING HEALTHY BOUNDARIES WHILE BEING EMPATHETIC

- *Why boundaries matter for emotional well-being*
- *Common misconceptions about empathy and limits*
- *Communicating needs kindly*
- *Sustaining empathy without burnout*

CHAPTER 15: HOW EMPATHY SHAPES OUR COMMUNITIES

- *The ripple effect of small acts of kindness*
- *Empathy in neighborhood groups and local events*
- *Schools, health services, and workplaces as centers of care*
- *Practical steps for strengthening communal ties*

CHAPTER 16: EMPATHY'S IMPACT ON LEADERSHIP

- *Building trust and loyalty through empathetic leadership*
- *Active listening and emotional awareness in decision-making*
- *Creating inclusive and supportive team cultures*
- *Balancing empathy with tough choices*

CHAPTER 17: EXERCISING EMPATHY FOR PERSONAL GROWTH

- *How empathy reveals personal blind spots and biases*
- *Developing resilience and self-confidence*
- *Deepening relationships and discovering new interests*
- *Finding purpose through caring for others*

CHAPTER 18: PRACTICAL EXERCISES TO STRENGTHEN EMPATHY

- Daily micro-practices and reflection activities
- Perspective-taking and emotional awareness methods
- Collaborative group exercises at home or work
- Turning empathy-building into lasting habits

CHAPTER 19: TEACHING EMPATHY TO OTHERS

- Guiding children, students, coworkers, and friends
- Modeling and praising empathetic behavior
- Overcoming barriers like fear, time limits, and skepticism
- Creative, digital, and real-world approaches to teaching empathy

---

CHAPTER 20: CREATING A MORE EMPATHETIC FUTURE

- Envisioning a society built on respect and kindness
- The roles of education, policy, technology, and grassroots efforts
- Practical steps for personal action and global change
- Sustaining empathy across generations

Chapter 1: What Is Empathy?

Empathy is our ability to understand and share the feelings of another person. When we show empathy, we do more than just hear the words someone is saying—we try to sense what is going on inside them. We feel their emotional state, and we respond with understanding and care. That might mean we offer support, a hug, a kind word, or just a listening ear. Empathy is like a bridge between people, helping us stay connected on a deeper level.

But empathy isn't just about being "nice." It is also about seeing and appreciating someone else's point of view. When we make an effort to step into another person's world, we break away from our own perspective. We notice that others have their own worries, joys, struggles, and triumphs. This realization helps us treat them with greater kindness and understanding. We see them as humans who feel things, just like we do.

Many people think empathy is the same as sympathy. But there is a difference. Sympathy is about feeling sorry for someone who is going through a hard time. Empathy goes a step further by trying to actually feel what that person feels. We attempt to place ourselves in their shoes. This doesn't mean we always agree with them or that we take on their emotions in a harmful way. Instead, it means we recognize that what they are feeling is real, and we respect that.

Empathy is also different from pity. Pity often creates a divide where you might see yourself as better off or above the other person's suffering. Empathy brings people on the same level, so we can truly understand each other as equals. It is a powerful tool that helps us connect, even if we come from different backgrounds or disagree on certain things.

The Building Blocks of Empathy

Empathy is often thought of as a skill, not just a trait you are born with. Like any skill, it can be improved with practice. It involves:

1. **Awareness**: You first need to notice someone else's feelings or emotional state. This can be done by observing body language, tone of voice, and even the words they choose when speaking.
2. **Understanding**: After you notice, you try to make sense of it. Ask yourself, "What might they be feeling right now?" "Why are they feeling

like this?" "Is there something going on in their life that is causing this emotion?"
3. **Emotional Connection**: This is the step where you consciously try to imagine yourself in their position. It's like picturing yourself in their situation and feeling what they might be feeling.
4. **Response**: Finally, empathy involves giving a response that shows you understand. This might be offering words of encouragement, a gentle touch, or simply listening without judgment. The main goal is to show them that you truly "get" their experience.

In many ways, empathy is a skill that blends the mind and the heart. The mental part is your ability to think about what another person is going through. The emotional part is when you feel that person's feelings as if they were your own. Practicing both parts can help you become better at empathizing.

Why Is Empathy Important?

Empathy does not just help the person who is hurting. It also helps the person who is showing empathy. When you show care and understanding, you can build stronger relationships. People learn they can trust you and open up to you. They see that you care, and this makes them feel safe. Over time, your relationships can grow deeper and more meaningful.

Empathy can also reduce conflicts. When we understand why someone does what they do, we are less likely to judge them harshly. For example, if you have a coworker who is often short-tempered, it can be easy to get mad back. But if you know that this coworker is under great stress at home, you might respond with patience and offer help instead of anger. This doesn't mean you excuse bad behavior; it simply means you understand where it might be coming from.

When people are empathetic, they tend to be less lonely, because empathy encourages connection and support. Feeling heard and understood gives people a sense of belonging. This is true in friendships, romantic relationships, families, workplaces, and even larger communities.

Empathy in Everyday Life

Empathy isn't just used in big moments like comforting someone after a loss. It can be shown in small, everyday interactions. For example:

- **Listening to a friend**: When a friend is talking about their day, really pay attention. Notice how they feel, not just what they say. If they mention being stressed or sad, encourage them to say more about it. Let them feel safe to share.
- **Resolving small conflicts**: When you disagree with your partner or sibling, try to see why they think the way they do. This does not mean you have to agree, but understanding their point of view can help you find a solution or at least reduce the tension.
- **Helping strangers**: If you see someone struggling with groceries, you can offer to help. This small act shows you see that they might need help, and you care enough to do something about it.
- **Being present on social media**: Even online, you can use empathy. Instead of leaving a rude comment when you disagree with someone, try to understand their side. You can ask questions rather than make assumptions.

Over time, these small acts of empathy can make a big impact. They shape the way people see you and feel about themselves. They also add positivity to your community.

Understanding Ourselves Through Empathy

One of the surprising things about empathy is that it can help you understand yourself better. When you practice trying to see how other people feel, you also become more aware of your own emotions. You become more mindful of what triggers your feelings and how you respond to different situations. This self-awareness can help you better manage your own reactions, making you more understanding and calm.

People often underestimate this part. We think of empathy as focusing on the other person's experience. But empathy and self-awareness go hand in hand. When you are aware of your own emotions, you can better notice when those emotions might block your ability to empathize. For example, if you are stressed or anxious, you might not have the mental space to notice someone else's needs. By knowing and managing your own stress, you keep yourself open to connecting with others.

The Science Behind Empathy

While we are not diving deep into complex science or fancy language, it is helpful to know that many studies show empathy plays an important role in how we socialize. Our brains have special cells called "mirror neurons" that seem to help us "mirror" the feelings and actions of others. When you see someone smile, these neurons light up, and you might feel a hint of their happiness. Likewise, if you watch someone stub their toe, you might instinctively wince as if you felt some of their pain.

Though science is always learning more about how exactly empathy works in the brain, it is clear that empathy is not just an imaginary concept. Our brains are wired to connect with and care about others. This helps us survive and build meaningful bonds.

How Empathy Looks Different in Different People

Just as people have different personalities, they also have different ways of showing empathy. Some might be quick to hug and console a crying friend. Others might show empathy through quiet acts of service, like cooking a meal or spending time with someone who is sad. Some people are more talkative and can say the right words to comfort someone. Others are better at offering a calm presence. There is no single correct way to show empathy, but the core idea is the same: you sense how someone else feels, and you respond in a caring manner.

Some people are more naturally empathetic. They pick up on cues like facial expressions and tone of voice. Others need more practice. Either way, empathy can be grown over time. It is like a muscle that gets stronger with the right exercises. If you do not use it, it can weaken. If you keep practicing, it will become a bigger part of who you are.

Summary

Empathy is the ability to sense and understand another person's feelings. It involves awareness, understanding, emotional connection, and a supportive response. It is different from sympathy and pity, because empathy puts you on equal ground with the other person. Empathy matters because it helps us feel closer to others, solves conflicts, and brings more kindness into everyday life. It can be practiced in small moments and big ones, and it also helps us understand ourselves better.

In the chapters that follow, we will dig deeper into why empathy matters in our daily lives and how we can make it a stronger part of who we are. You do not need fancy words or theories to grow your ability to empathize. You just need an open heart, a willingness to learn, and the desire to treat people with care. It might seem challenging at first, but as you will see, empathy can change not only your life, but the lives of those around you, too.

Chapter 2: Why Empathy Matters in Our Daily Lives

Empathy might sound like a soft or optional trait, but it is actually a big part of how we get along with others. It affects how we communicate, solve problems, and even how we feel about ourselves. Think about how many times a day you interact with people—at home, at work, in public, or online. Each interaction can go better if there is empathy involved. Let's explore why empathy truly matters in our day-to-day life and how it shapes our attitudes, relationships, and choices.

Building Stronger Relationships

1. Deepening Bonds
When you show that you really understand someone's feelings, you create a sense of closeness. This closeness helps friendships grow because people feel safe talking to you. They trust that you will not judge them. Over time, this can lead to long-lasting friendships or more meaningful relationships with family members.

2. Reducing Misunderstandings
Many arguments happen because we make assumptions about what the other person is thinking or feeling. Empathy pushes us to pause and see things from their side. By asking, "How are they really feeling right now?" or "Why might they be reacting this way?" you can avoid jumping to conclusions. This simple step can save both parties a lot of hurt or anger.

3. Fostering Mutual Respect
When you empathize with someone, you show them respect. You acknowledge their feelings and experiences as valid. In turn, people often respond with greater respect and understanding toward you. This creates a positive loop where both sides treat each other better and better over time.

Helping with Communication

1. Listening Better
Empathy naturally improves your listening skills. Rather than waiting for your turn to talk, you focus on what the other person is saying and how they feel. This

can lead to fewer misunderstandings and deeper, more productive talks. People often feel relieved just by being heard.

2. Choosing the Right Words
When you care about another person's feelings, you try to avoid saying things that will cause unnecessary harm. Empathy encourages you to think before you speak. You might say something like, "I see you're upset about this. Let's figure this out together," instead of "Stop complaining." This small change in wording can keep a conversation calm and helpful, rather than hurtful.

3. Strengthening Nonverbal Cues
Communication is not only about words. Facial expressions, body language, and tone of voice carry a lot of meaning. When you are empathetic, you pay closer attention to these signals, and you become more careful about the signals you give in return. A gentle tone or a sincere smile can let someone know you truly care.

Easing Conflict and Stress

1. Seeing the Bigger Picture
When you take the time to understand someone else's viewpoint, you are less likely to get stuck in your own anger or frustration. This can be especially helpful in high-stress situations, like a dispute at work or a tense family gathering. Empathy helps you step back and think, "We are all humans here, with our own reasons for feeling how we feel."

2. De-escalating Tension
Empathy can calm down heated situations. Imagine someone is really upset about a delayed project deadline. If you respond to them by saying, "I can see this has been stressful for you. Let's see how we can fix this," you validate their feelings and show you want to help. This can often diffuse anger or hurt more effectively than a defensive reply would.

3. Encouraging Cooperation
When people see that you care about their feelings, they are more likely to work with you, not against you. In a team setting, empathy can boost cooperation because team members feel valued and understood. This often leads to better outcomes, as more people will share ideas and try to find joint solutions.

Increasing Emotional Well-Being

1. Feeling Connected
One of the biggest human needs is to feel connected to others. When you practice empathy, you create chances for connection. You also receive empathy in return over time, which builds an emotional support system for everyone involved. Feeling understood is a key part of happiness and emotional health.

2. Promoting Self-Awareness
As mentioned before, empathy is linked to self-awareness. When you try to understand others, you also reflect on your own feelings and behaviors. You become more mindful of how your words and actions affect the people around you. This can encourage a healthy level of self-examination, leading to personal growth.

3. Decreasing Loneliness
Empathy can help reduce feelings of isolation. When people empathize with you, you realize that you are not alone in how you feel. In turn, when you empathize with others, they do not feel alone either. This shared humanity can help everyone feel a little less lonely, which is especially important in times when people feel isolated or disconnected.

Creating Positive Communities

1. Spreading Kindness
Empathy can be contagious. When you show empathy, people notice and may pass that empathy on to someone else. Simple acts, like asking a neighbor how they are doing or supporting a friend in need, can spread kindness throughout a group or community. Over time, empathy can become part of a community's culture.

2. Encouraging Volunteering and Helping
Communities that value empathy often have higher rates of volunteering. People see the struggles of others and are moved to help. They may organize food drives, fundraisers, or simply spend time helping someone learn new skills. All of these efforts strengthen the community and give people a sense of purpose.

3. Building Bridges Between Different Groups
Empathy allows us to see that different backgrounds, lifestyles, or beliefs do not

have to divide us. When we make an effort to understand people who seem "different," we often find common ground. This can reduce prejudice and bring people together to solve common problems or just enjoy each other's company.

Guiding Better Decisions

1. Considering the Impact on Others
When you choose to do something, empathy encourages you to think about how it will affect those around you. This might be a personal decision, like moving to a different place, or a group decision, like setting policies in a business. By including empathy in the decision-making process, you are more likely to treat people fairly and kindly.

2. Making Ethical Choices
Empathy helps you become more ethical because you see beyond your personal gains. You understand that your actions can either help or harm others. This mindset can guide you toward choices that are not just good for you, but also for the people around you and society at large.

3. Improving Leadership
Leaders who practice empathy tend to be more liked and respected. They listen to the concerns of their team, they make space for different opinions, and they consider the well-being of the people they lead. This often results in better teamwork and higher morale. People feel heard and know their leader cares about them.

Empathy's Role in Health

1. Emotional Health
Feeling understood and cared for can reduce stress, anxiety, and depression. When we share our burdens and realize someone genuinely understands, it can ease some of our emotional pain. This is a big reason why supportive counseling, therapy, and peer support groups help people. Empathy is at the core of all these approaches.

2. Physical Health
Believe it or not, empathy can also have a positive effect on physical health. Chronic stress and feeling alone can harm your body. When people feel supported and understood, their stress levels often decrease, which can help

with things like blood pressure and heart health. While empathy is not a cure-all, it can certainly contribute to a healthier lifestyle.

3. Medical Settings
In hospitals and clinics, empathy from doctors and nurses can make a huge difference. Patients who feel cared for often have a smoother recovery and feel less anxious. When a healthcare worker takes time to understand a patient's fears or concerns, the patient is likely to feel safer and more willing to follow treatment plans. This can lead to better health outcomes.

Overcoming the Challenge of Modern Life

In modern life, we are often busy, stressed, and surrounded by digital distractions. It's easy to forget the importance of connecting deeply with people. However, empathy might be more important now than ever before.

1. Technology and Empathy
While technology allows us to stay connected across great distances, it can also lead to shallow interactions. Social media, text messaging, and other forms of digital communication can strip away the tone, facial expression, and body language that help us express empathy. This means we have to make a conscious effort to insert empathy into our online interactions, whether that is by using kind words, thoughtful questions, or video calls where we can see each other's faces.

2. Stress and Empathy
The faster life moves, the harder it can be to slow down and consider someone else's feelings. Yet empathy can actually help relieve our own stress. When we understand each other better, we reduce the confusion and tension that often lead to conflicts. Taking a moment to show care can transform a stressful day into a more positive experience.

3. Global Connection
Our modern world is more connected than ever. We can talk to people from different cultures and backgrounds with a few clicks. Empathy helps us bridge differences in language, tradition, and belief. By seeing each person as a fellow human with real feelings, we can learn to work together to solve global challenges, from climate issues to social injustice.

Making Empathy Part of Your Daily Routine

Now that we have explored many ways empathy matters, you might wonder how to make it a daily habit. Here are some simple tips:

1. **Start Small**: Pick one interaction a day where you consciously try to understand someone's feelings. This could be a conversation with a coworker, a cashier, or a family member.
2. **Ask Questions**: Instead of guessing how someone feels, ask them. Use open-ended questions like, "How did that make you feel?" or "What has been bothering you the most?"
3. **Listen and Reflect**: Practice active listening. Reflect back what you heard: "It sounds like you had a really rough day," or "So you're feeling nervous about the meeting next week." This helps the other person know you truly heard them.
4. **Observe Nonverbal Cues**: Notice people's facial expressions, posture, and tone of voice. This will help you understand when they are upset, tired, or excited, even if they do not say so in words.
5. **Give Thoughtful Responses**: Based on your observations, try to respond in a way that shows understanding. If someone is sad, a simple, "I'm sorry to hear that. Is there anything I can do?" can be more comforting than you might imagine.
6. **Reflect on Yourself**: After an interaction, ask yourself how it went. Did you truly connect? Did you learn something about the other person's feelings? Self-reflection helps you improve your empathetic skills over time.

Conclusion

Empathy matters in our daily lives because it touches every aspect of how we connect with other people. It helps build stronger relationships, improves our communication skills, reduces conflicts, and fosters a sense of belonging. It also supports our emotional and physical well-being. In a fast-paced and sometimes impersonal modern world, empathy serves as a glue that holds individuals and communities together.

By choosing empathy each day—both in big ways and in small acts—you make a real difference in the lives of the people around you. In return, you often find yourself feeling more supported, understood, and valued. The good news is that empathy can be learned, practiced, and strengthened. You do not need special talent or fancy words to be empathetic. You only need a genuine desire to understand and care.

In the chapters ahead, we will explore more specific areas of empathy, like the different types of empathy and how to recognize and overcome the blocks that sometimes stop us from being empathetic. We will also look at how body language, culture, and digital communication all play roles in empathy. The journey may take time and effort, but it is a journey well worth taking. By committing to growing your empathy, you not only improve your own life, but you also help create a kinder, more understanding world.

Chapter 3: Different Kinds of Empathy

Empathy is not a single, one-size-fits-all skill. People often talk about empathy as if it is one simple idea, but in truth, there are different ways empathy can show itself. Being aware of these different kinds of empathy can help you better understand your own reactions and learn how to respond more compassionately to others. In this chapter, we will take a closer look at these different forms of empathy and how they appear in everyday life.

---

1. Emotional Empathy

What It Is
Emotional empathy is when you feel someone else's emotions almost as if they are your own. You see a friend crying and suddenly you also feel a wave of sadness. You hear good news from a coworker, and you feel a surge of joy in your own heart. Emotional empathy can feel strong because it creates a direct link between another person's emotional state and your own.

Real-Life Examples

- **Watching a Sad Movie**: When you watch a movie where the main character suffers a big loss, you might find tears welling up in your eyes. You are sharing in their sadness, even though you know it is just a story.
- **Seeing a Friend in Pain**: If your friend has had a rough day, you might notice your mood shifts to match theirs. You feel heavy or drained, reflecting their sorrow.

Benefits

- **Deep Emotional Connections**: Because you truly feel what others are going through, it can create a strong sense of closeness.
- **Comfort and Support**: Emotional empathy can help you sense when someone needs a hug, a shoulder to lean on, or simple reassurance.

Drawbacks

- **Emotional Overload**: If you take on the feelings of many people around you—especially negative ones—it can be overwhelming. You might struggle to separate your own feelings from those of others.

- **Burnout**: People who have strong emotional empathy sometimes end up emotionally drained if they do not take breaks or set boundaries.

---

2. Cognitive Empathy

What It Is
Cognitive empathy is about understanding another person's emotions or perspective on a more mental level. Instead of fully feeling what the other person feels, you make a mindful effort to see the situation from their point of view. This kind of empathy is often related to problem-solving and communication skills because it allows you to "think" like someone else without necessarily absorbing their emotions.

Real-Life Examples

- **Workplace Discussions**: When trying to solve a conflict with a coworker, you might try to see why they are upset about a certain policy or decision. You put yourself in their situation mentally.
- **Negotiations**: Mediators or negotiators often use cognitive empathy to figure out what the other side needs or wants. This insight helps find solutions that work for both parties.

Benefits

- **Clearer Thinking**: Because cognitive empathy does not sweep you up in strong emotions, you can keep a level head. This often helps in problem-solving.
- **Better Communication**: You can speak in a way that connects with the other person's viewpoint. This can help reduce misunderstandings.

Drawbacks

- **Lack of Emotional Warmth**: Relying too much on cognitive empathy alone might make you seem distant or cold. You are understanding the person's feelings logically, but they might still feel you are not "truly" there for them in an emotional sense.
- **Manipulation Risk**: In rare cases, someone who is good at cognitive empathy but lacks compassion might use that understanding to manipulate others.

3. Compassionate Empathy (Also Called Empathic Concern)

What It Is

Compassionate empathy is often described as the best blend of emotional and cognitive empathy. You not only understand what someone is feeling and share in their feelings to some degree, but you also have a strong desire to help. In other words, you feel moved to take action. This is empathy that is guided by kindness, care, and a true wish to improve the other person's well-being.

Real-Life Examples

- **Volunteering**: You see people in need—maybe they lack food or shelter—and you feel compelled to do something about it. So you volunteer your time or resources.
- **Helping a Grieving Friend**: When a friend loses a loved one, you sense their sadness, think about what they might need, and then step in with helpful gestures like cooking a meal or organizing support from others.

Benefits

- **Positive Impact on Others**: Because you turn empathy into action, you create real change. You ease someone's struggles, even if just a little.
- **Personal Growth**: Taking action can give you a sense of purpose, reminding you that empathy can be a powerful tool for good.

Drawbacks

- **Emotional Weight**: Acting on someone else's problems can be time-consuming or emotionally heavy. You might need to manage your own energy carefully.
- **Frustration**: When you cannot fix a situation (like a big social problem or a crisis that is beyond your control), you may feel helpless or upset.

4. Somatic Empathy (Physical Empathy)

What It Is

Somatic empathy is less commonly talked about, but it involves physically feeling what someone else feels in your own body. This does not mean you literally get injured when they do. Rather, you might experience similar physical sensations—like feeling tension, aches, or a sense of warmth—when you see or sense someone else's discomfort or emotions.

Real-Life Examples

- **Feeling a Tightness in Your Chest**: You might feel your own chest tighten when you watch someone else suffer from anxiety or panic, even though you are not actually the one in that situation.
- **Mirror Pain**: Sometimes, when you see someone stub their toe or cut their finger, you may feel a quick jolt of pain or a shudder in your own body.

Benefits

- **Heightened Awareness**: Somatic empathy can serve as an alarm that alerts you to another person's stress or pain before they even say anything. This can help you respond faster.
- **Deeper Understanding**: Feeling something physical can make the other person's experience more "real" to you.

Drawbacks

- **Physical Stress**: If you are very sensitive to other people's pain or stress, you can end up with your own physical discomfort, which can be draining.
- **Boundary Problems**: People with strong somatic empathy need good boundaries. Otherwise, they might end up carrying bodily stress that does not belong to them.

---

5. The Role of Culture and Upbringing

How we develop and show different kinds of empathy can depend a lot on our culture and how we were raised. Some cultures place a high value on emotional expression, so emotional empathy might be more common or more accepted. Other cultures may encourage people to keep their emotions private, leading people to rely more on cognitive empathy—discussing feelings in a calm, logical way.

Our families also shape how we use empathy. A parent who consoles a child through hugs and verbal comfort may teach that child the value of emotional empathy. Another parent might praise the child for thinking through a classmate's situation, emphasizing cognitive empathy skills. As we grow up, these early lessons can guide how we respond to others.

6. Balancing Different Kinds of Empathy

In practice, we often blend more than one kind of empathy. For example, you might start by logically trying to understand a coworker's frustration (cognitive empathy), then find yourself feeling some of their stress (emotional empathy), and finally decide to help (compassionate empathy). None of these kinds of empathy are "right" or "wrong." Each has strengths and potential downsides.

Tips for Balance

1. **Know Your Limits**: If you are someone who strongly feels others' emotions, remember to take care of yourself. That might include taking breaks, journaling, or talking with a friend or therapist.
2. **Stay Aware**: Pay attention to whether you are leaning too heavily on logic and not giving enough emotional support—or vice versa. A little self-reflection after tough situations can help you adjust.
3. **Practice Compassionate Empathy**: Whenever possible, see if you can add a helping action to your understanding or shared feeling. Even small acts can make a big difference.
4. **Reflect on Motivations**: Ask yourself, "Am I really trying to help the other person, or am I making it about me?" Genuine empathy focuses on the other person's needs, not your need to appear caring.

7. Situational Use of Different Empathy Types

The kind of empathy you use often depends on the situation. Here are a few examples:

- **Crisis Situations**: Imagine someone is in an emergency, like they lost their home in a fire. Emotional empathy might let you feel their shock and fear, but cognitive empathy can guide you on practical steps they need—such as finding temporary housing or contacting insurance. Finally, compassionate empathy can motivate you to actually take those steps and offer help.
- **Workplace Conflicts**: Sometimes, showing too much emotional empathy can make a tense situation more confusing if you become upset, too. In these moments, a balanced approach—using cognitive empathy to see why each person is upset, then following up with supportive language—can be more productive.
- **Personal Relationships**: If a close friend shares a painful loss, emotional empathy (feeling their pain) often helps them feel understood on a deeper level. Then, you might use compassionate empathy to offer real-life support or just stay with them so they are not alone.

---

8. Can People Learn New Types of Empathy?

Yes, empathy is a skill that can be practiced and developed. If you find it easy to understand people on a logical level but struggle to really feel their emotions, you can practice noticing body language and tone of voice. Try to imagine the last time you felt a similar feeling. This helps you shift into a more emotional type of empathy.

On the other hand, if you get easily overwhelmed by emotions, it can help to focus on the "why" behind someone's feelings. This more cognitive approach can keep you from feeling overrun by their emotions. Then, once you understand the situation, you can decide how to respond with kindness or action without losing yourself in someone else's pain.

---

9. Why Does It Matter?

Understanding the different forms of empathy helps us become more flexible in how we deal with others. Sometimes, the best way to help a person is simply to feel with them (emotional empathy). Other times, they might need a calm, practical approach (cognitive empathy). And often, they need a blend of both, plus some active help (compassionate empathy).

Also, being aware of these different empathy types can stop you from being too hard on yourself if you do not always feel strong emotions when someone else is upset. Maybe your strength lies in calmly guiding them through a problem. Or you might be the one who can share deep feelings easily but needs some help taking the next step to solve the issue. Neither approach is wrong—you can always learn to balance and grow more types of empathy over time.

---

10. Summary

Empathy comes in several forms, each with its own strengths and weaknesses:

1. **Emotional Empathy**: Sharing someone else's feelings directly.
2. **Cognitive Empathy**: Understanding someone else's perspective or feelings on a mental level.
3. **Compassionate Empathy**: A caring mix of feeling, understanding, and a desire to help.
4. **Somatic Empathy**: Physically sensing the stress, pain, or emotions of others in your own body.

No one type is "better" than the other. The key is to recognize when a certain type of empathy is most helpful or most fitting to a situation. By practicing and balancing these different forms, you can deepen your connections and respond to others in a way that truly supports them. In the next chapter, we will look at what can block empathy from flowing and what we can do to overcome those obstacles. Understanding these blocks will help us avoid the pitfalls that can stop us from connecting with others in a genuine way.

Chapter 4: Blocks to Empathy and How to Overcome Them

As we have seen, empathy can be a powerful way to connect with others. But sometimes, we find it hard to step into someone else's shoes. We might even realize that we are pulling away from their feelings. There are many reasons empathy can get blocked. It could be due to personal stress, cultural biases, mental exhaustion, or plain misunderstanding. In this chapter, we will explore the most common blocks to empathy and discuss ways to break them down.

---

1. Stress and Overwhelm

What It Is
One of the most common blocks to empathy is our own stress or overwhelm. When we are going through a rough time—like dealing with financial worries, family problems, or health challenges—we have limited emotional energy to spare for others.

How It Blocks Empathy

- **Tunnel Vision**: We become so focused on our own problems that we do not notice someone else's feelings or needs.
- **Emotional Exhaustion**: Our mental space is already used up by our troubles, leaving little room to feel or understand someone else's emotions.

How to Overcome

1. **Self-Care**: Take breaks, find ways to relax, and keep track of your mental health. This might include taking a quiet walk, meditating for a few minutes, or even talking to a therapist.
2. **Set Boundaries**: If you are drained, it is okay to tell someone, "I want to help, but I need a little time to clear my head first." This keeps you from offering empty support when you are not really able to.

3. **Seek Help**: If your stress is constant and overwhelming, share your burden with a friend, counselor, or other trusted person. Reducing your own stress load opens up space for you to empathize again.

---

2. Cultural or Personal Biases

What It Is

Biases are preconceived ideas or judgments we make about certain groups or individuals. These can come from our upbringing, social groups, media, or personal experiences. When we carry biases—either conscious or unconscious—we might quickly judge people rather than try to understand them.

How It Blocks Empathy

- **Stereotyping**: We assume we already know what a person is like based on their race, gender, religion, or background, so we do not bother to learn how they feel.
- **Dehumanizing**: In extreme cases, biases can make us see certain people as "less" human or less deserving of compassion.

How to Overcome

1. **Self-Awareness**: The first step is to recognize you have biases. Everyone does. Pay attention to when your mind jumps to a negative assumption about someone.
2. **Educate Yourself**: Seek out stories, books, or conversations with people from different backgrounds. Personal exposure helps break down stereotypes.
3. **Challenge Quick Judgments**: When you catch yourself thinking, "They are all like that," pause. Ask yourself if you really know that person's individual story. Force yourself to consider that each person is unique.
4. **Practice Humility**: Accept you do not know everything about other people's experiences. Stay open-minded and willing to learn.

3. Fear of Being Vulnerable

What It Is
Sometimes, we avoid being empathetic because we fear what it might bring up in ourselves. Empathy can require you to tap into your own feelings—especially ones that are painful or make you feel weak. You may worry that if you share someone's sadness, it will cause you emotional distress.

How It Blocks Empathy

- **Emotional Distance**: You keep a safe distance from other people's problems so you do not have to face the feelings within yourself.
- **Shutting Down**: You might cut people off or change the subject when they talk about something sad or troubling, because it hits too close to home.

How to Overcome

1. **Embrace Vulnerability**: Remind yourself that feeling sadness or pain from others is not a sign of weakness. It shows you care, and caring is a human strength.
2. **Build Emotional Resilience**: This might mean talking to a counselor, joining a support group, or journaling regularly about your feelings so you are less scared of them.
3. **Take Small Steps**: Practice empathy in safe, small doses. Offer a listening ear to a friend about a mild concern, then build up to more serious situations. Over time, you will see that empathy does not break you—it can actually help you grow stronger.

---

4. Lack of Time or Attention

What It Is
In our busy modern world, many of us rush from one task to another. Our minds are often racing, or we are glued to our phones. We might not notice someone's emotional signals because we are too distracted.

How It Blocks Empathy

- **Missed Cues**: You fail to see someone's tears, tense posture, or change in voice tone because you are looking at your phone or thinking about your to-do list.
- **Surface-Level Interactions**: You only have quick chats with people, never long enough to discover what they really feel.

How to Overcome

1. **Be Intentional**: Set aside time each day to be fully present with the people in your life. Put your phone away, turn off the TV, and make eye contact.
2. **Active Listening**: Practice focusing on someone's words and body language without interrupting. This does not take as long as you might think, but it does require focus.
3. **Check In**: Even if you are busy, a simple "How are you doing—really?" can open the door to empathy. Make time for deeper follow-up when needed.

---

5. Emotional Burnout or Compassion Fatigue

What It Is

This is common among people who spend a lot of time caring for others, such as nurses, social workers, teachers, or even family caregivers. When you constantly deal with other people's pain or needs, your own ability to empathize can start to wear down. You might become numb to their problems as a coping mechanism.

How It Blocks Empathy

- **Numbness**: You stop reacting with concern or even feeling emotional when you see someone suffering.
- **Irritability**: You might feel annoyed when someone needs help because you have little energy left to give.

How to Overcome

1. **Self-Care Routine**: Make self-care a non-negotiable part of your daily life. This might include enough sleep, balanced meals, and regular exercise.

2. **Support Systems**: Talk to colleagues or friends who understand what you are going through. Sharing stories and giving each other moral support helps reduce compassion fatigue.
3. **Set Realistic Limits**: Know when to step back. You cannot help everyone all the time. Setting boundaries and allowing yourself to say "no" can protect your emotional health.

---

6. Judgment or Moral High Ground

What It Is
Sometimes, we block empathy because we judge the other person's choices or lifestyle. We think, "They brought it on themselves," or, "I would never do that." We then fail to see their pain because we are focused on deciding if they are "right" or "wrong."

How It Blocks Empathy

- **Blame Game**: By focusing on blame, we forget to see the person's humanity.
- **Lack of Compassion**: Even if a person did make mistakes, that does not mean we cannot feel for their situation.

How to Overcome

1. **Shift Your Mindset**: Move from "They should have known better" to "They are human and they hurt just like I do."
2. **Remember Your Own Mistakes**: Think about times you made poor decisions and felt regret or pain. This can help you relate to someone else's struggle.
3. **Use Compassion, Not Judgment**: You do not have to agree with someone's actions to feel empathy for their situation.

---

7. Competition or Comparison

What It Is
In some settings—like competitive workplaces or sibling rivalries—people see

each other as rivals rather than fellow humans with feelings. You might be too focused on winning, beating a target, or proving you are better.

How It Blocks Empathy

- **Seeing Others as Obstacles**: You view colleagues or siblings only as competition, not as people who might have fears, joys, or personal challenges.
- **Jealousy**: If you envy someone's success, you may not want to empathize with them, especially if they are struggling. You might even think they "deserve" the hardship.

How to Overcome

1. **Team Mindset**: Even if you are in a competitive field, see how cooperating at times can be beneficial. Recognize the human element in your rivals.
2. **Focus on Personal Growth**: Instead of comparing yourself to others, aim to be a better version of yourself. This leaves space to empathize rather than resent.
3. **Find Common Ground**: Whether through shared hobbies or life experiences, finding similarities can make you see the person behind the competition.

---

8. Lack of Self-Empathy

What It Is
Strangely enough, a lack of self-compassion can also block empathy for others. If you are harsh on yourself—never allowing yourself to feel sad or tired—you might expect the same from others. You might not understand why someone is overwhelmed or needs emotional support because you refuse to give that kindness to yourself.

How It Blocks Empathy

- **Hard Expectations**: You think, "If I can handle it without complaining, so should they."
- **Emotional Blindness**: Ignoring your own feelings leads to ignoring the feelings of others.

How to Overcome

1. **Practice Self-Compassion**: When you make a mistake or feel down, treat yourself like you would treat a friend. Offer supportive words instead of criticism.
2. **Recognize Human Limits**: We all have limits. Admitting your own struggles helps you see that others might struggle too.
3. **Allow Emotions**: Give yourself permission to feel sad, angry, or worried sometimes. This helps you do the same for other people.

---

9. Technology and Digital Barriers

What It Is

In our online world, we often communicate through screens. Texts, social media posts, and emails can lose the tone, face-to-face contact, and emotional cues that real-life interactions give us.

How It Blocks Empathy

- **Impersonal Communication**: Without seeing someone's face or hearing their voice, it is easy to forget there is a real person with real feelings on the other side of the screen.
- **Online Anonymity**: People may say hurtful things online that they would never say face to face, reducing empathy.

How to Overcome

1. **Use Video or Voice When Possible**: If you need to have a serious or emotional conversation, try to do it in person or through a video call, where you can see and hear each other.
2. **Think Before You Type**: Before sending a text or posting a comment, ask yourself how it might affect the other person.
3. **Mindful Browsing**: Recognize when you are getting overwhelmed or desensitized by too many online stories. Take breaks to reset.

10. Strategies for Rebuilding Empathy

We have touched on specific tips for each block, but here are some overall strategies to keep empathy flowing:

1. **Develop Emotional Awareness**: Spend a few moments each day checking in with your own feelings. This helps you be more aware of others' emotions, too.
2. **Improve Communication Skills**: Practice active listening, asking open-ended questions, and rephrasing what the person said to ensure you understand them.
3. **Engage in Empathy Exercises**: For example, take a moment to imagine what it feels like to be in a situation that someone else is describing.
4. **Seek Diverse Interactions**: Talk to people outside your usual social circle. Different cultures, ages, and backgrounds can teach you new perspectives.
5. **Practice Mindfulness**: Being present in the moment can help you notice emotional cues. If your mind is always elsewhere, you will miss signs that someone needs support.
6. **Reflect on Your Actions**: After a day of interactions, think about moments where empathy might have been missing. How could you have responded differently?

---

11. Knowing When Empathy Is Not Enough

It is also important to remember that there are times when empathy alone may not fix the problem or heal someone's pain. While empathy is a powerful force, some situations need professional help, like therapy or medical treatment. Being empathetic does not mean you have to fix everyone's problems by yourself. Sometimes, the best way to show empathy is to guide someone toward the right resources or encourage them to seek professional support.

12. Summary

Empathy can be blocked by many factors, such as stress, biases, fear of vulnerability, or simply a lack of time and attention. Understanding these blocks is the first step to overcoming them. By learning to care for ourselves, challenging our own biases, and being more present in our interactions, we can remove the barriers that keep us from truly understanding and caring for others.

The path to becoming more empathetic is not always easy. It takes effort to look inward, to acknowledge our flaws, and to practice the skills that make empathy possible. But when we do this work, we create a world where people are seen, heard, and valued. As we move forward in this book, we will keep exploring ways to build empathy and apply it in different areas of life. In the next chapters, we will discuss how body language and active listening techniques can shape empathy in more direct, practical ways. Understanding these skills will help us break down any remaining barriers and become better at connecting with others on a deeper level.

Chapter 5: The Role of Body Language in Empathy

When we think about empathy, we often focus on our words and thoughts. We try to understand how someone else feels and sometimes imagine ourselves in their place. But there is another powerful way to show and sense empathy: **body language**. Our posture, facial expressions, and gestures can communicate volumes about how we feel and whether we truly care about the person in front of us. Likewise, reading another person's body language can help us know how they feel—even when they do not say it out loud.

In this chapter, we will discuss how body language shapes empathy. We will look at how you can improve your understanding of nonverbal cues, how you can use your own body language to build trust and closeness, and what pitfalls to avoid. By the end, you will have a clearer view of how to "listen" not just with your ears, but with your eyes and entire presence.

---

1. Why Body Language Matters for Empathy

Beyond Words
People do not always say exactly how they feel. Sometimes they are scared to admit they are hurting. Sometimes they are not even sure how they feel themselves. But their body language might still reveal clues. A person's hunched shoulders might show worry. Rapid tapping of the foot might signal impatience or tension. A soft, relaxed posture might show contentment. By picking up on these signals, you can respond more accurately to someone's emotional state.

Building Trust
When people see that your posture and facial expressions match your supportive words, they feel safer opening up. On the other hand, if you say, "I'm here for you," but you stand with your arms crossed and avoid eye contact, the other person might not believe your words. Consistency between what you say and how you show it is key. Trust grows when actions and words line up.

Bridging Communication Gaps
Body language can help bridge language barriers or cultural differences—though

we do need to be cautious, as gestures can mean different things in different cultures. Still, human expressions like smiling or frowning are fairly universal. A warm, welcoming posture often feels safe to people from many different backgrounds. When words fail or do not tell the whole story, body language can fill the gap.

---

2. Common Types of Body Language

There are many forms of body language. Here are some of the most common and how they might shape empathy:

1. **Facial Expressions**: A raised eyebrow can show surprise or doubt. A furrowed brow can show confusion, sadness, or concern. Slight changes in someone's mouth—like pursed lips—might signal worry or disapproval. Being aware of these subtle changes can help you see what the other person might be feeling.
2. **Eye Contact**: Looking into someone's eyes (in a respectful way) often shows you are paying attention. It can also tell you a lot about how they feel. People who are sad or ashamed might look down. Someone who is angry might have a fixed, intense stare.
3. **Posture**: How a person stands or sits can reveal emotions. A slouched posture might show tiredness or sadness. Standing up tall, with shoulders back, often signals confidence or determination. Leaning in during a conversation usually indicates interest. Leaning away might show discomfort or fear.
4. **Gestures**: These can be hand movements, nods, or head shakes. For instance, a small nod can show that you are listening or that you agree. A quick head shake can tell someone you disagree or do not understand. Some gestures are universal, like shrugging for uncertainty, but others can vary by culture.
5. **Touch**: A gentle pat on the back, a handshake, or a light touch on the arm can communicate support and concern. Of course, touch should always be used carefully and respectfully—some people do not like being touched, and cultural norms can differ. Still, a kind, well-timed touch can offer a lot of comfort.
6. **Tone of Voice**: Although tone of voice is not exactly "body" language, it is closely linked. How you say something can matter as much as what you

say. A soft, calm tone often shows empathy. A loud or harsh tone might show anger or frustration, even if the words themselves sound polite.

3. Reading Other People's Nonverbal Cues

Start with Observation
Building empathy through body language begins with noticing. Before jumping to any conclusions, simply observe the other person. Are they fidgeting? Looking away? Clenching their fists? Note these signs without rushing to guess what they mean.

Consider the Context
Context is everything. Crossed arms might mean the person is cold, or it might mean they feel defensive. Fidgeting might be a sign of anxiety, or it might just be a habit. To figure out which interpretation makes sense, think about what is happening in the situation. Are they in a tense meeting? Is the temperature in the room cold? Did something happen just before that might have triggered a certain feeling?

Look for Clusters
No single gesture or expression tells the whole story. If someone keeps yawning, it might not mean they are bored—it could mean they slept poorly. But if they are also checking their watch, glancing at the door, and leaning away, that might mean they are bored or anxious to leave. Body language often comes in clusters—multiple signs that together paint a bigger picture.

Ask, Don't Assume
If you see signs of discomfort, sadness, or anger, do not assume you know the reason. Instead, you can gently check in with the person. You might say, "I notice you seem a bit tense. Would you like to talk about what's going on?" This approach shows empathy and invites them to share, rather than putting words in their mouth.

4. Using Your Own Body Language to Show Empathy

Open Posture
When you want to show someone you are listening and care, keep your arms and legs uncrossed if possible. Face them directly. Lean in slightly. This makes you look approachable and engaged, which helps the other person feel safe to talk.

Maintain Appropriate Eye Contact
Making eye contact shows you are focused, but be mindful not to stare too intensely, as that can feel aggressive. A good balance is to look at the person's face enough to show attention, then occasionally look away or nod.

Relaxed Facial Expressions
Try to keep a calm, attentive expression. You can show concern by gently furrowing your brow if they are talking about something sad, or you can smile softly if they share good news. Be genuine—people can often sense a forced smile.

Nodding and Simple Gestures
If you agree or simply want to show understanding, a small nod can encourage the person to keep talking. You can also use your hands to make reassuring gestures, like a gentle wave, an inviting motion to keep going, or a slow, calm hand movement that signals "I hear you."

Matching Their Pace
Sometimes, matching someone's speaking pace or the general level of their energy can help them feel at ease. If they are talking quietly about a sad event, respond in a softer tone. If they are excited about something happy, allowing a little upbeat energy in your voice and posture can show you share in their excitement.

---

5. The Impact of Cultural Differences on Body Language

Varied Meanings
A gesture that seems harmless in one culture might be offensive in another. For example, direct eye contact is considered respectful in some cultures but can be seen as rude or challenging in others. Even personal space norms differ. In some places, standing close is normal, while in others, people keep more distance.

Listening to Learn
If you interact with people from different cultural backgrounds, it helps to do a little research about common gestures and norms. Even better, you can politely ask how they prefer to communicate. This shows respect and helps avoid misunderstandings.

Focus on Universal Expressions
Basic emotions like sadness, joy, fear, or anger often share similar facial expressions around the world. A genuine smile is usually understood as friendly, while crying or tearing up usually signals sadness or overwhelm. Pay attention to these universal cues, but keep in mind that people might still show or hide them differently based on their cultural upbringing.

---

6. Pitfalls to Avoid in Body Language

Overdoing It
Sometimes, in an attempt to show empathy, a person may exaggerate their body language—nodding too much, leaning too close, or staring intensely. This can make the other person uncomfortable. Subtle, genuine signals are usually best.

Being Distracted
Constantly checking your phone or glancing around the room sends a clear message that you are not fully present. Even if you are listening somewhat, the person might feel you are not truly there for them. Put distractions aside when you want to show empathy.

Mirroring Inappropriately
Mirroring someone's posture or gestures can help build rapport, but it must be done naturally. If you mimic them too obviously, it might seem you are mocking them. Let mirroring happen gently, if at all.

Ignoring Personal Space
Being too physically close can feel invasive. If you notice the person leaning away, take a small step back. Respect for personal space is vital to keep a conversation comfortable.

7. Body Language and Emotional Regulation

Sometimes, using empathetic body language can help you stay calm and supportive, even if you are upset or stressed. For instance, taking slow breaths, relaxing your shoulders, and maintaining a gentle facial expression can steady your own emotions. This in turn helps the other person feel calmer. In a tense situation, if you keep a friendly posture and relaxed tone, it can defuse anger or fear on both sides.

---

8. Exercises to Improve Body Language Awareness

Try these simple exercises to become more aware of both your own body language and that of others:

1. **Mirror Practice**: Stand in front of a mirror and try different facial expressions—happy, sad, confused, worried. Notice how your eyes, eyebrows, and mouth change. This can help you recognize these expressions in others.
2. **Silent Observation**: The next time you are in a public place—like a coffee shop—take a few moments to watch people interact, without listening in on their words (do not stare, just casually observe). Notice their posture, hand movements, and facial expressions. See if you can guess how they might be feeling.
3. **Posture Check**: Throughout the day, pause and check your posture. Are your shoulders tense or raised? Are you slouching? Straighten up, roll your shoulders back, and take a deep breath. Notice how it affects your mood.
4. **Record Yourself**: If you feel comfortable, record a short video of yourself talking about a simple topic. Watch it back. Notice if you look tense, fidgety, or relaxed. This can be eye-opening, as many people do not realize how they appear to others.
5. **Subtle Mirroring**: In your next friendly conversation, try to naturally mirror the person's posture once or twice—if they lean back, you might lean back a moment later. See if it makes the conversation feel more in sync.

9. Body Language in Group Settings

Empathy is not only one-on-one. You might be in a meeting or a group of friends where some people talk and others stay silent. Observing body language can tell you who might feel left out or who might be uncomfortable. If you see someone looking away or shrinking into their seat, you could politely invite them to share their thoughts. On the other hand, if someone looks like they have something urgent to say—maybe they are leaning forward or tapping their foot—you can notice and give them space to speak.

When you practice empathetic body language in a group, try to face people when they speak, nod to show understanding, and turn toward quieter participants to encourage them. This helps create a more inclusive environment.

---

10. Body Language Over Digital Communication

It can be harder to pick up on body language in digital communication, but video calls still offer many cues. Pay attention to facial expressions, posture, and eye movement on the screen. If someone keeps looking away, they might be multitasking or feeling uncomfortable. If they lean in and maintain eye contact with the camera, they are likely engaged.

When you speak, remember to look at the camera often (this helps simulate eye contact), keep your gestures within the camera's frame, and maintain a friendly expression. Although it is not the same as being in person, these small actions can still improve empathy in virtual interactions.

---

11. Putting It All Together

Body language is a key part of empathy because it helps us sense and show genuine concern, even when words do not tell the whole story. By paying attention to posture, facial expressions, gestures, tone of voice, and more, we can better understand what someone else is feeling. We can also adjust our own nonverbal cues to show that we care.

- **Observe**: Watch for clusters of signals rather than single gestures.

- **Respond**: Offer an open posture, calm eye contact, and matching tone.
- **Respect**: Stay mindful of personal space and cultural differences.
- **Check In**: If you notice someone's body language suggests distress, politely ask how they are doing.

Practicing these skills takes time, but the rewards are big: better connections, fewer misunderstandings, and a sense of closeness that words alone cannot always provide.

---

12. Summary

Body language forms a huge part of our interactions. When we use our eyes, face, and body with care and genuine intent, we can create deeper empathy. We can also spot signs of sadness, stress, or happiness in others and respond in a supportive way. The key is to be observant, stay respectful of differences, and match our nonverbal cues with our empathetic intentions. In the next chapter, we will explore **Active Listening Techniques**, which go hand in hand with understanding body language. Together, these skills create a strong foundation for building true empathy in our everyday lives.

Chapter 6: Active Listening Techniques

Listening is a big part of empathy. It goes beyond simply hearing the sounds another person makes. True, **active listening** means giving your full attention, taking in not just the words but also the emotions behind them, and showing the speaker that you understand what they are saying. Many of us think we are good listeners, but in truth, we often listen passively. We let our minds wander, or we jump in with our own thoughts before the other person finishes. In this chapter, we will look at what active listening is, why it matters, and how to practice it in daily life.

---

1. What Is Active Listening?

Hearing vs. Listening
Hearing is a physical process—your ears pick up sounds. Listening, though, is a mental and emotional process. You focus on what the other person is communicating and try to understand their viewpoint. With active listening, you are not just passively letting words wash over you. You are engaged, curious, and genuinely interested in what they have to say.

Being Present
Active listening requires being fully present in the conversation. You put aside distractions—like your phone or wandering thoughts—and give the speaker your attention. You also show you are present by making eye contact (if appropriate), nodding, and using small verbal confirmations like "I see," or "Uh-huh," in a calm, encouraging tone.

Empathetic Understanding
At its core, active listening is about empathy. You want to see the world through the speaker's eyes, at least for the moment. Even if you do not agree, you try to understand how they feel and why. This helps the other person feel heard, which can be a huge relief when they are stressed, sad, or just need to share.

---

2. The Benefits of Active Listening

1. **Reduced Misunderstandings**: When you listen carefully, you make sure you fully grasp what the other person means before you respond. This cuts down on confusion or arguments based on false assumptions.
2. **Deeper Relationships**: People who feel heard tend to open up more. Trust grows when you show you are genuinely interested in someone's feelings or opinions.
3. **Better Problem-Solving**: By truly hearing someone's concerns, you can work together more effectively to find solutions. You are also more likely to uncover the root of an issue.
4. **Less Conflict**: Active listening can defuse tension. Sometimes, a person just needs to vent and feel understood. When you let them do so without interrupting or judging, the tension may decrease.
5. **Personal Growth**: Active listening can help you learn from others. You might discover new viewpoints or ideas that can expand your own thinking.

---

3. Key Steps in Active Listening

Step 1: Focus Your Attention

- Clear your mind of distractions.
- If possible, put your phone on silent or away from you.
- Face the person. Make eye contact if it feels comfortable for both of you.
- Notice their body language and tone of voice.

Step 2: Avoid Interrupting

- Let the speaker finish their thought.
- Even if you have a question or comment, hold it until they pause.
- This shows respect and allows them to express their full idea without feeling cut off.

Step 3: Use Verbal and Nonverbal Feedback

- Nodding, small smiles, or "Mm-hmm" can reassure them you are following along.

- Be mindful of your own facial expressions—show understanding, not judgment or boredom.
- Keep your tone calm and supportive.

Step 4: Paraphrase and Clarify

- After they finish a main idea, repeat back or summarize what you heard in your own words. For example: "So you're feeling worried about your job because of the recent changes, right?"
- Ask clarifying questions if something is unclear: "When you say 'recent changes,' do you mean the new management policy?"
- This step helps ensure you understand their meaning and shows them you are really listening.

Step 5: Validate Their Feelings

- This does not mean you must agree with everything they say, but you can acknowledge their emotions.
- Phrases like, "It sounds like that was really tough for you," or "I can understand why you'd feel upset," go a long way in showing empathy.
- Validating feelings helps the speaker feel respected and heard.

Step 6: Offer Thoughtful Responses

- Only after they have fully expressed themselves and you have clarified, you can offer your perspective, advice, or additional thoughts—if they ask for it.
- Sometimes, people just want to be heard and do not need advice right away. Ask if they want input: "Do you want me to help brainstorm a solution, or do you just need me to listen?"

---

4. Barriers to Active Listening

Internal Distractions
These are thoughts in your own mind that pull you away, like worrying about your own tasks or daydreaming. To overcome this, pause, take a deep breath, and refocus on the speaker.

Emotional Reactions
If you strongly disagree with what the speaker is saying, or if it triggers your own feelings, you may become defensive. Remind yourself to listen first before reacting. You can always share your view after you fully understand theirs.

Over-Eagerness to Help
Sometimes we jump in with solutions too soon because we want to fix the problem. But if you do this too fast, the speaker may feel cut off or that you are not really trying to understand. It is better to get the whole story before offering advice.

Habitual Interrupting
Some people grew up in environments where conversations involved talking over one another. Breaking that habit might take practice. Consciously note how often you interrupt. If you catch yourself doing it, apologize and let the speaker continue.

---

5. Techniques to Deepen Your Listening

Reflective Statements
After the speaker talks about a situation, repeat the gist of it back to them in your own words. For instance, "It sounds like you feel alone in this project because no one is helping you." This helps them see you are trying to get it right and gives them a chance to correct you if you missed something.

Open-Ended Questions
Rather than asking "yes" or "no" questions, use open-ended ones. "How did that make you feel?" or "What was that like for you?" This invites them to share more details and feelings, which helps you understand deeper.

Check for Accuracy
Before you respond with your own story or idea, you can ask, "Did I get that right?" or "Is that how you feel?" This quick check can prevent misunderstandings.

Empathetic Silence
Sometimes the best support is silence. Allow pauses in the conversation. Let the speaker think, reflect, or even gather the courage to share more. Rushing to fill

every quiet moment can interrupt their flow of thought or push them to change the subject prematurely.

6. Active Listening in Different Contexts

1. Family and Friends

- In personal relationships, active listening can foster closeness and trust.
- Offer your loved ones a safe space to talk about their problems or joys without judgment.
- Simple statements like "I'm here for you, please tell me more" can be powerful.

2. Workplace

- Whether you are a manager or a team member, actively listening can improve communication and reduce mistakes.
- When coworkers feel heard, they are more likely to cooperate.
- In meetings, pay close attention instead of scrolling through your phone or checking email.

3. Conflict Situations

- When tensions are high, active listening can defuse anger.
- By calmly letting the other side air their grievances, you show respect, which may lower defenses.
- Paraphrasing their concerns without judgment can help them see you as a fair listener.

4. Helping Roles

- Counselors, volunteers, or anyone in a helping profession often rely on active listening.
- People who are struggling may need more than quick advice—they need to feel truly understood.
- Even if you are not a professional helper, using active listening skills when a friend is in crisis can be a lifesaver.

7. Tips for Overcoming Common Challenges

Challenge 1: Wanting to Share Your Own Story
It is natural to relate someone's story to your own experiences. Sometimes that can be helpful. But be mindful: if you jump in too soon with "Oh, that same thing happened to me!" it might sound like you are making it about you. Instead, try to let them finish, confirm their feelings, and then see if they want to hear about your similar experience.

Challenge 2: Running Out of Time
In a busy day, you might feel you do not have time to listen properly. If it is a serious matter, try to schedule a time when you can give them your full attention. Or let them know you care but want to talk properly later: "I want to hear all about this. I'm a bit short on time right now. Can we chat tonight?"

Challenge 3: Feeling Triggered by Their Topic
Sometimes, someone's story might trigger your own painful memories or strong reactions. If that happens, take a deep breath and notice your emotions. If it is too intense, you can gently say, "I'm sorry, but I'm feeling overwhelmed right now. I might need a moment." It is better to pause and regroup than to pretend you are okay and then shut down emotionally.

Challenge 4: Dealing with a Repetitive Speaker
Some people talk in circles or repeat the same complaints. It can feel draining to keep listening. In these cases, try to reflect back and clarify their main concern: "I hear you saying that you are upset about X, Y, and Z. Is there anything new you'd like to add, or are these the main issues?" You might also set gentle limits while still being empathetic: "I want to support you, but I also notice we keep coming back to the same points. Maybe we can think about what can be done next, or if we should talk to someone who can help us find a solution."

---

8. Activities to Practice Active Listening

1. Listening in Pairs
Ask a friend or family member to practice with you. Pick a topic—could be something small like a funny story. One person speaks for two or three minutes without interruption. The other person listens quietly, then summarizes or

reflects what they heard. Switch roles. Notice how it feels to be listened to without interruption.

2. Listening Journal
After talking to someone about an important topic, write down what you remember. What was their main concern? How did you respond? Did you interrupt? This helps you see where you can improve.

3. Delayed Response
In your next conversation, force yourself to count two seconds in your head after the speaker stops talking before you reply. This small pause can stop you from jumping in too fast and give you time to process what they said.

4. Practice with Media
Watch a short interview or podcast. Then pretend you are going to paraphrase and validate the speaker's feelings. Think about what open-ended questions you might ask if you were there in person.

---

9. The Role of Body Language in Active Listening

Active listening and body language go hand in hand. While you focus on their words, keep an empathetic posture: face them, maintain gentle eye contact, and nod occasionally to show you are with them. Keep your arms in a relaxed, open position, and lean in slightly. If you notice the speaker getting emotional, show care through your expression or a soft, understanding tone. These nonverbal signals reinforce your verbal message: "I care about what you are saying."

---

10. Knowing When Active Listening Is Enough (and When It's Not)

Active listening is powerful, but it cannot solve every problem. Sometimes people might need more help—like professional therapy, medical attention, or financial assistance. Your role can be to listen and acknowledge their pain. Then, if you see the issue is beyond what empathy alone can handle, encourage them to reach out for the help they need. Offering a listening ear is a beautiful start, but some problems need more than that. Being honest about your limits is also part of healthy empathy.

11. Summary

Active listening is a cornerstone of empathy. By focusing on the speaker, avoiding interruptions, reflecting on what is said, and validating their feelings, you build trust and understanding. This skill improves relationships in families, friendships, workplaces, and beyond. It helps reduce conflict, leads to better problem-solving, and creates a sense of being truly heard. But it requires practice and patience—especially in a busy world full of distractions.

Remember:

- **Be Present**: Set aside distractions and really focus.
- **Listen First, Then Respond**: Let them share fully, then offer paraphrasing, validation, or advice only if they want it.
- **Stay Curious**: Ask open-ended questions and clarify to make sure you understand.
- **Respect Boundaries and Time**: Sometimes you need to schedule a better time to talk.
- **Body Language Matters**: Show with your posture and expression that you care.

By combining active listening with the lessons from the previous chapter on body language, you create a solid foundation for empathy. You learn not only to hear what people say, but also to sense what they might feel underneath. The more you practice these skills, the more natural they will become, and the stronger your empathetic connections will grow.

In the next chapters, we will shift our focus to more specific situations where empathy plays a key role—like romantic relationships and the workplace. Applying active listening in these areas can bring about huge improvements in communication and closeness. You will see that empathy, supported by strong listening and nonverbal cues, can transform how we connect with each other in many parts of life.

Chapter 7: Empathy in Romantic Relationships

Romantic relationships often bring feelings of love, excitement, and closeness. But they can also be challenging. One of the most important tools for keeping these relationships healthy and warm is **empathy**. When partners make an effort to see and feel things from each other's point of view, they build a strong bond of understanding and trust. Empathy can help solve conflicts, deepen emotional connection, and promote respect between partners.

In this chapter, we will discuss why empathy matters so much in romantic relationships, explore ways to practice empathy with your partner, and look at some common pitfalls to avoid. We will also talk about how to handle disagreements and how empathy can help couples grow closer over time.

---

1. Why Empathy Is Important in Romantic Relationships

Emotional Connection
When you care deeply for someone, you want them to feel loved and understood. Empathy helps you do this by tuning in to their emotions. Whether your partner feels happy, sad, worried, or excited, being empathetic shows you truly notice and share in what they are experiencing.

Reducing Misunderstandings
Many fights in romantic relationships happen because one person thinks the other doesn't care or isn't listening. When you practice empathy, you show you're paying attention, which cuts down on confusion. Instead of jumping to conclusions, you try to get a clear picture of how your partner feels, helping avoid arguments that stem from guesswork.

Building Trust
Trust grows when both people believe the other person respects and cares about their well-being. Empathy says, "I'm here, and I see what you're going through." This lets your partner know you're on their side. Over time, consistent empathetic actions make the relationship feel stable and safe.

Supporting Each Other's Growth
Couples evolve over time. Jobs change, families expand, health can shift, and

personal interests can move in new directions. Empathy helps you support each other's changing needs and dreams. When one partner feels understood, they're more open to sharing their hopes, worries, and plans for the future.

---

2. Practical Ways to Show Empathy to Your Partner

1. Ask Genuine Questions
Take the time to ask, "How are you really feeling today?" or "What was the toughest part of your day?" These open-ended questions give your partner room to share more than just "I'm fine." Listen closely to the answers and follow up. For instance, if your partner says, "I'm stressed about work," ask, "Is it the workload, or is something else bothering you?"

2. Reflect What You Hear
When your partner shares a concern, show you understand by reflecting their words. For example, if they say, "I'm worried I'm not performing well at my job," you could respond, "So you feel pressured at work, and you're worried about meeting expectations. Is that right?" This step helps them know you truly caught what they said.

3. Validate Their Feelings
Even if you don't agree with your partner's point of view, you can still validate their feelings. You might say, "I can see why that would make you upset," or "That sounds like it would be scary." Validation doesn't mean you think they're right about everything; it just means you acknowledge that their emotions are real and matter.

4. Offer Help, But Don't Overstep
Sometimes the best way to show empathy is to ask, "Is there anything I can do to support you?" Wait for your partner's answer. They may need advice or practical help. Or maybe they just need a hug. By asking, you avoid assuming you already know the best way to help.

5. Use Nonverbal Cues
Look your partner in the eye when they speak (if that's comfortable for both of you), nod, and keep an open posture to show you're listening. You can also place a gentle hand on their shoulder or hold their hand if it feels right. These small actions can show emotional support.

3. Handling Disagreements With Empathy

No relationship is without conflict. But empathy can change the way conflicts unfold. Instead of a harsh exchange, an empathetic argument aims to understand the other person's viewpoint, even in the heat of the moment.

Step 1: Pause and Breathe
When tensions rise, it's easy to say hurtful things. Before reacting, take a slow breath. This small pause can help you stay calm enough to listen fully. Remind yourself, "I care about this person, and I want to see why they feel this way."

Step 2: Listen Without Defending
Let your partner explain their side before you jump in. Try to see if there's any truth to what they are saying. You can think, "Is there a part of their concern I can understand or agree with?" If so, acknowledge it.

Step 3: Reflect Their View
Summarize what you heard. For example, say, "I hear you saying that you feel I haven't been helping around the house much. You're frustrated and feel like you're doing all the work alone." Then ask if you got it right.

Step 4: Share Your Perspective Gently
After you've shown you understand their point, share your feelings: "I see how stressed you are. I've also been feeling exhausted from longer hours at work, and I think that's why I've been forgetting to help. But I recognize that's not fair to you." This balanced approach shows you respect your partner's view while still expressing your own concerns.

Step 5: Look for a Win-Win
Empathy isn't about letting your partner walk all over you. It's about working together to find a solution that feels good to both of you. If chores are the problem, maybe you can set up a clear schedule or divide tasks differently. The main point is to solve the problem as a team, not to defeat each other.

4. Empathy and Emotional Support

Being a Safe Haven

In a healthy romantic relationship, each partner can be a safe place for the other's emotions. This means not judging or belittling them when they open up. If your partner comes to you with fears or doubts, try to offer warmth and understanding first, rather than criticism or a "quick fix."

Listening to Understand, Not to Reply

Sometimes, when our loved ones share troubles, we rush into giving advice. While advice can be helpful, many people first need to feel truly heard. Practice listening fully before giving your input. Ask if they want help finding solutions or if they just need a listening ear.

Respecting Different Coping Styles

Everyone deals with stress in different ways. Some people want to talk it out. Others need some alone time to think. If your partner needs space, try not to take it personally. Let them know you're there whenever they're ready to talk. Likewise, if you need space, explain that you aren't shutting them out—you just need to clear your head first.

---

5. Obstacles to Empathy in Romantic Relationships

Even if we care about each other, certain factors can block empathy:

1. **Stress and Exhaustion**: Long work hours or personal worries can sap our energy. We might have little patience left for listening or caring.
2. **Past Hurts**: If there have been betrayals or unresolved fights in the relationship, it might be harder to be open and empathetic. Trust can be damaged, making you less willing to see things from your partner's view.
3. **Unspoken Expectations**: Sometimes, we expect our partners to just "know" what we need without telling them. When they don't, we feel hurt. But if we haven't shared our needs clearly, empathy has less chance to grow.
4. **Fear of Vulnerability**: Opening up can be scary. Some people shut down because they worry they'll be rejected or mocked. This can make empathy

from the other person much harder, since they don't know what's really going on.

---

6. How to Bring More Empathy into Your Relationship

Check In Daily
A simple question like, "How was your day?" followed by real listening can keep you tuned in. Even just ten minutes of focused conversation, without phones or TV, can keep emotional closeness alive.

Express Appreciation
Don't wait for big moments to thank or praise your partner. Notice the small things they do. Saying "I really appreciate you washing the dishes today" or "Thanks for taking care of the kids while I worked" shows you see their efforts and respect them.

Share Your Feelings First
If you want your partner to open up, it can help if you lead by example. Maybe share something that made you happy or upset recently. This can encourage them to share their own feelings, setting a tone of openness.

Learn Each Other's Love Languages
The concept of "love languages" suggests people show and receive love in different ways—like words of affirmation, acts of service, gifts, quality time, or physical touch. While not everyone fits neatly into one category, talking about how you each prefer to give and receive love can improve empathy. You learn what makes your partner feel valued and can act accordingly.

Take Breaks in Conflict
If you feel an argument is getting out of control, it's okay to say, "Let's pause this for a moment, I need a little time to calm down." Then come back to the issue when you're both in a calmer state. This approach helps preserve empathy by avoiding heated outbursts.

7. Knowing When Outside Help Is Needed

Empathy can solve a lot of relationship challenges, but sometimes problems run deeper. Past traumas, ongoing misunderstandings, or major trust issues might require professional help. Couples counseling or therapy can offer a safe space for both partners to be heard. A trained counselor can guide you in learning new communication and empathy skills. Seeking help isn't a sign of a failing relationship—it can be a sign that you both care enough to try your best to make it work.

---

8. Empathy for Yourself, Too

Romantic empathy doesn't just flow one way. You also need to show empathy toward yourself. If you're feeling guilty or upset, treat yourself with kindness instead of harsh criticism. When you practice self-empathy, you're better able to give empathy to your partner. Otherwise, you might be too drained or stressed to care for someone else's feelings.

Setting Boundaries
Empathy doesn't mean ignoring your own needs. Sometimes, if a relationship is harmful or one-sided, you need to step back and protect your well-being. Healthy empathy respects both partners' emotions and needs—it's not all give for one person and all take for the other.

---

9. Growing Closer Through Empathy Over Time

Empathy in romantic relationships isn't a one-time event. It's a continuous process that evolves as you both change and face new life challenges. By regularly checking in, actively listening, and showing care, you weave a pattern of empathy that can strengthen your connection for years to come.

Milestones and Changes
Major life events—like moving, getting married, having kids, losing a job, or facing health issues—can put a lot of stress on a couple. Approaching these moments with empathy helps both people adapt better. Understanding that your

partner might be scared or uncertain can prevent fights and encourage teamwork.

Shared Goals
Couples who share or discuss their goals often find it easier to empathize when times get tough. If you both have a clear picture of what you're working toward—whether it's building a family, traveling the world, or saving for a house—you're more likely to support each other. You understand that struggles aren't personal attacks; they're bumps in the road to a shared future.

Everyday Moments Matter
Finally, empathy isn't just about big, serious talks. It shows up in everyday acts: a kind text during the day, noticing when your partner seems tired and making them tea, or offering encouragement if they feel down. These small moments of care stack up and create a strong emotional safety net.

---

10. Summary

Empathy is a key piece of any healthy romantic relationship. It allows partners to truly see, hear, and value one another. By asking genuine questions, reflecting and validating emotions, and avoiding blame, couples can handle disagreements in a kinder way. Regular check-ins, expressions of appreciation, and understanding each other's needs help keep empathy alive day by day.

No relationship is perfect, and empathy doesn't solve every issue instantly. But it paves the way for deeper communication, trust, and respect. When you prioritize empathy, you create a nurturing environment where both you and your partner can grow. If challenges become too big, it's wise to seek outside help, which can guide you toward healthier communication patterns. Remember, empathy also involves caring for yourself, so you have the emotional resources to share with your loved one. In the next chapter, we will explore how empathy can work in a very different setting: **the workplace**. Though professional relationships are not the same as romantic ones, empathy still has a vital role to play there, too.

Chapter 8: Empathy in the Workplace

When people talk about empathy, they often think about personal relationships—like family, friends, or romantic partners. But empathy also belongs in professional settings. After all, many of us spend a large portion of our day at work, interacting with colleagues, bosses, or clients. Fostering empathy at work can lead to better teamwork, reduced conflicts, and a more positive atmosphere. It can even boost productivity, because people who feel understood and respected are more motivated and engaged.

In this chapter, we will explore how empathy plays out in the workplace, discuss practical ways to show empathy as both an employee and a leader, and look at how cultural differences, remote work, and other factors can influence empathetic communication.

---

1. Why Empathy Matters in the Workplace

Improved Communication
When employees and managers practice empathy, they listen carefully before responding, which helps to avoid misunderstandings. If someone is struggling with a workload, an empathetic manager might ask, "What's going on?" instead of assuming laziness. This opens the door to honest discussion and problem-solving.

Better Teamwork
Teams function best when members trust and respect each other. Empathy helps you see that your coworker might be under pressure, dealing with personal issues, or just having an off day. When you step into their shoes, you become more supportive, which makes collaboration smoother.

Higher Job Satisfaction
People who feel valued and heard at work are generally happier. They are more likely to stay in their job rather than leave for another company. This lowers turnover and helps teams build long-term expertise and camaraderie.

Conflict Resolution
Arguments in the workplace can get tense if both sides only want to prove they

are right. Empathy encourages everyone to pause and ask, "How does the other person see this situation?" That question alone can cool heated tempers and lead to fair compromises.

Positive Reputation
An organization known for treating employees with understanding and empathy is more attractive to potential hires. It also helps with public image and can improve customer relationships. Customers often prefer dealing with companies that show genuine care.

---

2. Showing Empathy as an Employee

1. Offer a Helping Hand
If a coworker is overwhelmed with tasks, see if you can help without neglecting your own responsibilities. For example, if you have free time, volunteer to take on a small piece of their project. This gesture shows you notice their stress and want to support them.

2. Listen Actively in Meetings
Instead of waiting for your turn to speak, focus on what others are saying. This means setting aside your phone or laptop, making eye contact, and summarizing what people say if needed. If someone seems nervous presenting an idea, you can encourage them by nodding or asking clarifying questions.

3. Respect Work Styles
Not everyone works the same way. Some people are faster at certain tasks or prefer quiet environments. Others enjoy group brainstorming. Empathy means understanding these differences without labeling them as "good" or "bad." You can try to adapt your style when collaborating or at least be patient with how others operate.

4. Avoid Gossip and Judgment
Talking behind someone's back can create a toxic environment. If a coworker is struggling, try to understand what they are going through rather than spreading rumors. If you truly have concerns, it might be more empathetic to talk privately with them or with a supervisor in a constructive way.

5. Give and Receive Feedback Gently
Feedback is part of work life, but it can sting when delivered poorly. When giving feedback, focus on the task rather than personal traits. Say, "I noticed the report had a few data errors. Maybe we can double-check the numbers next time?" instead of "You're careless." When receiving feedback, try to stay open-minded. Even if it feels unfair, you can ask clarifying questions and see if there's anything useful you can learn.

---

3. Showing Empathy as a Leader or Manager

1. Know Your Team
A good leader invests time in understanding the strengths, challenges, and life situations of their team members. This doesn't mean prying into personal details. It means noticing if someone has a new baby at home and might be short on sleep, or if someone seems shy in group settings but excels in one-on-one tasks.

2. Be Approachable
Keep your office door open if possible, or let your team know you're happy to schedule chats. Encourage them to share concerns early, so small problems don't become big ones. When you seem open and caring, employees feel safer coming to you with honest feedback or requests for help.

3. Listen to Ideas
Leaders who shut down ideas without consideration can crush morale. Even if an idea is not perfect, hearing it out with respect and empathy can encourage creativity. You can say, "That's an interesting thought. Let's explore how it might work," instead of "No, that's never going to happen."

4. Support Work-Life Balance
Some employees might have personal responsibilities, like caring for children or elderly parents. Empathy means being flexible with schedules if possible, or at least showing understanding if someone occasionally has to leave early. The better balanced employees feel, the more likely they are to stay committed and productive at work.

5. Praise and Acknowledge Effort
A leader who only points out mistakes misses a chance to inspire. Recognize achievements, even small ones, like meeting a deadline or solving a tricky

problem. A simple "thank you" or "great job" can go a long way in making people feel valued.

---

4. Managing Conflicts with Empathy

Workplace conflicts can arise from clashing personalities, misunderstandings, or competition for resources. Empathy can help resolve these in a healthier way.

Step 1: Listen to Each Side Separately
If you're a manager, let each person share their side of the story privately. Be careful not to blame or shame them. Your goal is to understand how each person perceives the situation.

Step 2: Look for the Core Issues
Are they arguing about a project deadline, or is there an underlying tension—like feeling disrespected or overshadowed? Sometimes, the real issue goes deeper than what's being said on the surface.

Step 3: Bring Them Together
In a calm setting, have them talk and listen to each other's viewpoints. Encourage them to reflect back what the other person said, just like you would in active listening. This can help them see if they misunderstood each other.

Step 4: Work Toward a Fair Solution
Aim for a solution that addresses the main concerns both people have. Maybe they can share tasks differently or agree to clearer communication channels. The goal is not just to "split the difference," but to find a path both can accept.

Step 5: Follow Up
After the conflict, check in with both parties. Are they keeping to the agreement? Have tensions eased? Ongoing empathy helps prevent the conflict from flaring up again.

5. Cultural and Generational Differences

Respect for Diversity
Modern workplaces are often diverse. People from different cultures, age groups, or backgrounds might have different communication styles. Empathy involves respecting these differences rather than forcing everyone to behave the same way.

Cultural Norms
In some cultures, direct eye contact is a sign of respect; in others, it can feel aggressive. Some might prefer straightforward feedback; others might find it rude. Being aware of these differences helps you tailor your approach so that it lands well with each person.

Generational Gaps
Age differences can also affect work preferences. Younger employees might prefer quick text messages or chat apps, while older employees might lean toward face-to-face talks or emails. Empathy in this context means understanding each generation's comfort zone and not mocking or dismissing their style.

---

6. Remote Work and Empathy

Challenges of Working Remotely
With more people working from home or in different locations, we lose the face-to-face contact that can build empathy easily. Body language is harder to read over a video call, and written messages can be misread if the tone isn't clear. Some workers might feel isolated or lonely.

Empathetic Remote Communication

- **Use Video Calls (When Possible)**: Seeing faces can help you sense how your colleagues feel.
- **Check In Regularly**: A quick message asking, "How's your day going?" can keep relationships warm.
- **Respect Time Zones and Schedules**: If people are scattered across regions, be mindful of sending messages at odd hours.

- **Be Clear in Writing**: Add a friendly greeting or a polite closing to emails or chat messages. This small touch shows you care.

Building Team Culture Online
Leaders and teams can plan virtual coffee breaks or casual check-ins. Sharing personal updates or having a fun "question of the day" can help people bond. Though it might feel awkward at first, these small efforts can create a sense of belonging for remote workers.

---

7. Signs of an Empathetic Workplace Culture

- **Open Communication**: Employees feel safe asking questions or sharing feedback without fear of punishment.
- **Team Support**: Team members help each other out when someone is swamped, instead of just watching them struggle.
- **Respect for Boundaries**: People understand that coworkers might have personal emergencies or mental health needs, and they show understanding.
- **Diverse Voices Heard**: People from different backgrounds get to contribute ideas, and those ideas are seriously considered.
- **Low Turnover**: Employees stick around because they feel valued and seen as humans, not just as "workers."

---

8. Overcoming Obstacles to Empathy at Work

Even with the best intentions, empathy can be hard to maintain in a fast-paced or high-stress environment. Some common obstacles include:

1. **Tight Deadlines and Pressure**: When everyone is rushing to finish tasks, there may be little time for personal check-ins or supportive talks.
    - *Solution*: Schedule brief team meetings that include a personal check-in. Even a few minutes can foster empathy.
2. **Hierarchical Structures**: In some workplaces, employees feel they cannot speak honestly to higher-ups.

- Solution: Leaders can invite feedback through anonymous surveys or open Q&A sessions, showing they truly want to hear from everyone.
3. **Fear of Appearing Weak**: Some people think showing empathy might be seen as soft or not "professional."
    - Solution: Normalize empathy by praising employees who show kindness and understanding. Emphasize that empathy leads to better outcomes.
4. **Cultural Barriers**: With many backgrounds in one office, sometimes misunderstandings happen due to language or cultural norms.
    - Solution: Provide training or workshops on cultural awareness. Encourage employees to ask respectful questions when they are unsure.
5. **Personal Biases**: We all have biases that might make us less empathetic toward certain coworkers.
    - Solution: Self-awareness and training can help us recognize and challenge these biases. Encourage open conversations about diversity and inclusion.

---

9. Practical Exercises to Grow Empathy in the Workplace

Exercise 1: Role Reversal
In a team meeting, take a hypothetical situation—like a conflict with a client—and have people switch roles. For instance, if someone usually deals with budgeting, ask them to "pretend" to be the marketing person. This helps everyone see problems from different angles.

Exercise 2: Empathy Rounds
Set aside a short weekly meeting for team members to share one challenge they faced that week (it can be small, like a tough phone call). The rest of the team listens actively, asks clarifying questions, and offers supportive words. This can build a habit of listening and understanding.

Exercise 3: Shadow a Coworker
If possible, spend a day or even a few hours observing what another person's job is like. Often, we don't realize the pressures or details someone else handles. Seeing their tasks firsthand can spark empathy.

Exercise 4: Give "Roses and Thorns"
At the end of a project or week, each team member shares a "rose" (something positive) and a "thorn" (a struggle). This invites open conversation about both successes and challenges. By hearing each other's "thorns," team members can better empathize with each other's difficulties.

---

10. The Future of Empathy at Work

As workplaces become more diverse, digital, and fast-moving, empathy is becoming even more important. Companies that prioritize empathy are likely to stand out as healthier, more innovative places to work. Employees will be looking for work environments where they feel valued and heard, and empathy can be the key to meeting that need.

Remote and Hybrid Models
Many companies are moving to remote or hybrid work setups, where employees split time between home and the office. Leaders will need to find ways to keep empathy strong in virtual spaces. This includes using technology wisely, maintaining regular contact, and making sure no one feels left out.

Empathy for Customers
Empathy doesn't stop with colleagues. Businesses that show real understanding toward customers often do better financially and build strong brand loyalty. When employees feel empathy at work, it becomes easier to pass that empathy on to customers.

---

11. Balancing Empathy and Professional Boundaries

It's important to remember that empathy at work doesn't mean letting your job or emotional well-being get crushed by others' demands. You can be caring while still having clear boundaries about your own workload, time, and personal space. If a coworker constantly leans on you to do their tasks, empathize with their stress but also gently remind them that you have your own responsibilities.

Similarly, managers can be empathetic without letting employees take advantage of leniency. The balance lies in listening, understanding, and then working together to find a fair solution for everyone involved.

---

12. Summary

Empathy in the workplace boosts communication, teamwork, and overall morale. When employees and leaders commit to understanding each other's viewpoints and feelings, tensions can ease, conflicts can be handled with respect, and people generally feel more satisfied in their roles. Whether you're a frontline worker or a CEO, showing empathy can transform daily interactions from cold transactions into supportive exchanges.

- **As an Employee**: Offer help, listen actively, and respect different styles.
- **As a Leader**: Be approachable, learn about your team, and support a healthy balance between work and personal life.
- **In Conflict**: Use empathy to see both sides, find root issues, and work toward fair solutions.
- **Across Cultures and Generations**: Stay open-minded to different communication styles and norms.
- **In Remote Settings**: Build connection through check-ins, video calls, and clear, friendly written communication.

By making empathy a habit, workplaces can become places where people actually want to be—places where employees feel valued, motivated, and able to bring their best selves to the job. In the next chapters, we'll look at other key areas of life where empathy matters, including **parenting** and **cultural differences**. As we continue, remember that empathy isn't limited to our personal lives or romantic bonds. It's a skill that can shape every human interaction for the better, including our 9-to-5 routines and beyond.

Chapter 9: Empathy and Parenting

Parenting can be one of the most rewarding and challenging roles in life. As parents, caregivers, or guardians, we do our best to meet our children's physical needs—food, shelter, safety—but it is just as important to meet their emotional needs. **Empathy** plays a big part in raising secure, emotionally healthy children. When parents take the time to see things from their child's point of view, they help their child feel understood, safe, and valued. Over time, that sense of being cared for can help a child grow into a confident, empathetic adult.

In this chapter, we will explore why empathy is crucial in parenting, how to practice empathetic listening with children of different ages, and the positive impact empathy can have on family life. We will also talk about common pitfalls, such as being too quick to judge or dismiss a child's feelings, and ways to correct these habits for a healthier parent-child relationship.

---

1. Why Empathy Matters in Parenting

Emotional Security
Children rely on caregivers for safety and comfort. When you respond to your child's feelings with empathy, you teach them they can count on you. They learn that their emotions, whether big or small, are valid. This builds a sense of security that becomes the foundation for their emotional development.

Healthy Brain Development
Many experts in child psychology say that consistent emotional support in early years can help shape a child's brain in positive ways. Children who feel understood and reassured can better manage their own stress and fears. Over time, this can reduce the risk of emotional problems later.

Learning Empathy by Example
Children learn how to treat others mainly by watching the adults around them. If they see you listening carefully, respecting feelings, and comforting others, they are more likely to do the same. Empathy is "caught" as much as it is "taught."

Better Communication
Kids sometimes struggle to express themselves in words. When you approach

them empathetically, you create a safe zone for them to share worries, joys, or confusion. This can prevent misunderstandings. It also helps children feel braver to speak up, because they know you will take their thoughts seriously.

2. Using Empathy with Children of Different Ages

Children's communication styles and emotional needs change as they grow. Adapting your empathetic approach can make a big difference.

Infants and Toddlers

- **Reading Nonverbal Cues**: Babies communicate mostly through crying, facial expressions, and body movements. Pay attention to these signs to figure out if they are hungry, tired, uncomfortable, or just need attention.
- **Soothing Touch**: Holding or gently rocking a crying baby can show empathy through physical closeness.
- **Calm Voice**: Even though they cannot understand words fully, your calm and warm tone helps them feel safe.

Preschoolers (Ages 3–5)

- **Active Listening**: Preschoolers start using words to share their feelings and ideas. Listen closely, make eye contact, and nod to show you care.
- **Naming Emotions**: Help them learn words like "angry," "sad," or "excited." When they are upset, you can say, "It looks like you're angry because we have to leave the park now."
- **Playing**: Join their world of make-believe. Pretend play can be a window into how they see things. By playing along, you show respect for their imagination.

Elementary School Children (Ages 6–10)

- **Ask Open-Ended Questions**: Instead of "Did you have a good day?" try, "What was the best part of your day, and what was the toughest part?" This encourages more sharing.
- **Validate Feelings**: If they are disappointed because they lost a game, say, "I understand you're upset. It's hard to lose when you tried your best." This teaches them it is okay to feel sad.

- **Guide Problem-Solving**: When they face conflicts with friends, use empathy to understand their view, then guide them in finding solutions. Let them brainstorm ideas so they learn to handle issues with care.

Tweens and Teens

- **Respect Their Independence**: Teenagers are figuring out their identity. They might push you away or say they do not need help. Empathy here means giving them some space while staying emotionally available.
- **Non-Judgmental Listening**: If they come to you with a concern—about friends, school stress, or self-image—hold back on lecturing. Show you understand how big their worries feel at this stage.
- **Reflect Their Feelings**: You might say, "It sounds like you're feeling really stressed about your exams. That can be tough." Let them know their feelings matter before jumping into advice.
- **Healthy Boundaries**: While empathy is crucial, do not forget you are still the parent. You can have rules while respecting their emotions. Saying, "I get that you want to stay out late with friends, but I worry about your safety," blends empathy with guidance.

---

3. Empathetic Listening at Home

Set Aside Distractions
When your child wants to talk, try to pause what you are doing—turn off the TV, set your phone aside—and give them your full attention. This small action sends a big message: "You are more important than my phone or the TV show."

Use Calm Body Language
Children pick up on your facial expressions. If you look angry or annoyed, they might close off. Keep a gentle expression, maintain relaxed posture, and avoid crossing your arms. Lean in slightly to show interest.

Encourage Them to Share
Some kids are shy or unsure if it is safe to open up. You can prompt them by saying, "You look a bit upset. Do you want to talk about it?" or "I'm here if you need me." Let them decide when they are ready to talk.

Reflect What They Say

To make sure you understand them correctly, repeat back what you heard. "So you felt left out when your friends played a game without you, right?" This gives them a chance to correct you if you misunderstood, and it shows you are really listening.

Avoid Quick Fixes

Sometimes kids just want to vent or feel understood. Jumping in with "Just do this!" might make them feel you are not taking their emotions seriously. Often, the best approach is to acknowledge their struggle first. You can say, "That sounds really tough," and then ask if they want help thinking of solutions.

---

4. Handling Tantrums and Emotional Outbursts

All children, especially younger ones, can have outbursts. They may scream, cry, or say hurtful things. While this can be stressful, an empathetic approach can make these moments easier.

Stay Calm

If you match their anger with your own, the situation can escalate. Take a deep breath. Tell yourself your child is having trouble handling a big emotion—they are not doing this just to upset you.

Get Down to Their Level

Physically kneel or sit so you are at eye level with them. This can feel less intimidating to them. In a calm voice, you might say, "I see you are really upset. Can you tell me what's making you feel this way?"

Name the Feeling

Help them identify what they feel: "Are you sad because it is time to leave the playground?" or "I wonder if you are angry because you wanted the toy right now." Naming the emotion can help a child feel understood and also teaches them words to express themselves later.

Set Limits

Being empathetic does not mean letting dangerous or hurtful behavior slide. If they are hitting or throwing things, it is okay to say, "I know you are upset, but we cannot hurt others. Let's find a safer way to calm down." You can guide them to a quiet corner or use a calming technique like deep breathing together.

Validate, Then Redirect
Once you have acknowledged their feelings, suggest a more appropriate reaction. For example: "It's okay to be angry. Next time, maybe we can use words instead of screaming, so I can help you faster."

---

5. Empathy and Discipline

Discipline is meant to teach children right from wrong and keep them safe, but it can sometimes turn into punishment without understanding. Empathy can help you keep discipline fair and balanced.

Teach, Don't Just Punish
When you discipline, try to explain the reason behind it. "You pushed your brother, and that hurt him. We do not hurt people, because it makes them feel scared or sad." This way, the child learns the impact of their actions rather than just feeling scolded.

Listen to Their Side
If they break a rule, find out what led them to do it. Were they angry, tired, feeling neglected? Understanding the "why" can help you prevent similar behavior in the future. It also shows your child you care about their feelings, even when you correct them.

Natural Consequences
If possible, allow the child to face the natural outcome of their behavior. For example, if they refuse to wear a coat, they might feel cold. This real-life lesson can be more powerful than a forced punishment. An empathetic approach might be, "I see you're cold now. Let's bring your coat next time."

Be Consistent and Kind
Children do best when they know what to expect. If you have set a rule (like a bedtime or limit on screen time), stick to it calmly. Gentle yet firm consistency can feel safer to a child than unpredictable reactions. Let them know you still love them, even if you disapprove of what they did.

6. Teaching Empathy to Children

Model Empathy in Daily Life
One of the best ways to teach empathy is by showing it yourself. If your child sees you comforting a friend or being respectful to a service worker, they learn these are normal, caring behaviors. They will pick up on your tone, words, and body language.

Encourage Empathetic Acts
Look for opportunities where they can practice kindness—like helping a sibling with homework, or asking a lonely classmate to play. Praise them when they show thoughtfulness. "I'm proud of you for sharing your crayons with Sarah, it made her happy!"

Use Stories and Books
Reading stories about different characters and asking questions like, "How do you think he felt when he lost his dog?" can expand your child's ability to see another's perspective. This can be done in simple storybooks for younger kids or more complex novels for older ones.

Role-Playing
If your child struggles with empathy in certain situations—like sharing toys—try a quick role-play. Let them act out how they might respond if a friend feels upset. This safe, playful practice helps them prepare for real interactions.

Community Involvement
Engaging in volunteer work as a family (like helping at a local shelter or picking up litter at the park) shows children how their actions can help others. This hands-on experience can make empathy feel real and meaningful.

7. Empathy in Different Family Situations

Single Parents
Raising kids alone can be stressful. Keep practicing empathy, but also remember to empathize with yourself. If you are too exhausted, it is hard to be emotionally

available. Reach out for support when needed—friends, family, or support groups. Your child benefits when you care for your own well-being, too.

Co-Parenting After Divorce
If you and your child's other parent are separated or divorced, disagreements can happen. Still, showing empathy toward your child's feelings about the situation is crucial. Try to avoid talking badly about the other parent in front of the child. Encourage them to share how they feel about moving between homes or celebrating holidays in a new way.

Blended Families
When new partners or stepsiblings join the family, children might feel insecure. Listening to their concerns without brushing them aside can ease the transition. Let them share worries like, "Will Mom love me less now that she has a new baby with her partner?" A gentle, empathetic talk can reassure them.

Grandparents or Extended Family as Caregivers
Sometimes grandparents or aunts and uncles play a major role. It can be challenging if older generations have different parenting styles. Focus on the child's well-being. Try to find common ground about discipline and emotional support so that the child receives consistent empathy.

---

8. Avoiding Pitfalls and Common Mistakes

Dismissing Emotions
Sometimes parents say things like, "You're fine, stop crying," or "That's not a big deal." This can shut down a child's ability to express themselves. They might feel that their emotions do not matter. Instead, try, "I see you're upset. Want to talk about it?" or "I know it's tough. I'm here to help."

Comparisons to Others
Phrases like, "Why can't you be more like your brother?" or "Your sister never does that!" can create jealousy and resentment. Focus on the child's behavior and feelings in the moment, not someone else's.

Hovering or Overprotecting
While empathy involves caring for your child's feelings, being overprotective can limit their chance to learn resilience. If they never experience disappointment or

frustration, they may struggle to handle it later. You can acknowledge their feelings—"That game is frustrating, isn't it?"—but still let them face small challenges on their own.

Inconsistent Reactions
Children can get confused if one day you comfort them for spilling milk, and the next day you yell at them for the same thing. While nobody's perfect, trying to maintain a steady, empathetic response teaches children how to handle accidents or mistakes calmly.

---

9. Long-Term Benefits of an Empathetic Parenting Approach

Stronger Parent-Child Bond
When children feel safe sharing their feelings, they tend to keep you close through all stages of life. That bond can last into their teenage years and beyond, leading to better communication and trust.

Emotional Regulation Skills
Children who grow up with empathetic parents often learn to manage their emotions more effectively. They see how to handle anger or sadness without harmful outbursts.

Higher Self-Esteem
Knowing that their feelings are valued can boost a child's self-worth. They learn that they matter, which can help them stand up for themselves respectfully as they grow older.

Positive Social Relationships
Kids who learn empathy at home usually do better in friendships and teamwork. They tend to be more understanding, listen better, and cooperate with others, whether at school or in extracurricular activities.

Carrying Empathy Forward
An empathetic upbringing can create a ripple effect. As children become adults and perhaps have children of their own, they pass on the empathy they received. This can help form more caring communities and, hopefully, a kinder world.

10. Summary

Empathy is a cornerstone of healthy parenting. By actively listening to children's feelings and experiences, validating their emotions, and guiding them with kindness, parents can foster deep emotional security. This helps children develop strong self-esteem, better communication skills, and the ability to empathize with others. It also strengthens the parent-child bond, making it more resilient to life's ups and downs.

The path to empathetic parenting is not always smooth. Life gets busy, and stress can get in the way. But even small, consistent moments of empathy—like truly listening when a child is sad or setting fair but firm rules—can make a huge difference. By adapting how you show empathy as children grow older, using empathy in discipline, and being mindful of different family structures, you can create a nurturing environment for your child's emotional growth. In the next chapter, we will see how empathy plays out across **cultural differences**, exploring how values, customs, and language differences can affect our ability to understand and connect with each other.

Chapter 10: Cultural Differences and Empathy

Modern society is made up of many cultures, languages, traditions, and values. Sometimes, when people from different cultures interact, misunderstandings occur simply because they see the world in different ways. **Empathy** can serve as a bridge across these cultural gaps, helping us understand and respect what feels foreign or strange to us. But practicing empathy across cultures is not always straightforward. We need awareness, open-mindedness, and a willingness to learn from each other.

In this chapter, we will look at how empathy can overcome cultural barriers, explore some common challenges (like stereotypes and language issues), and share ways to grow our cross-cultural empathy skills. Whether you are traveling overseas, working in a diverse office, or just meeting neighbors from different backgrounds, these ideas can help you better connect and understand.

---

1. What Do We Mean by "Culture"?

Culture involves the shared beliefs, customs, habits, values, and norms of a group of people. It can be shaped by things like nationality, ethnicity, religion, language, or region. Even within the same country, different subcultures might form—based on rural vs. urban life, for example, or different family traditions passed down over generations.

Visible vs. Invisible Culture
Some parts of culture are easy to see: food, clothing, music, or dance. Other parts are more hidden: the way people think about time, personal space, or polite behavior. When we talk about empathy and culture, it often involves understanding these "invisible" elements.

---

2. The Importance of Empathy in Cross-Cultural Interactions

Reducing Prejudice and Stereotypes
When we see people from another culture only through a limited lens—perhaps based on media images or a single story we heard—we risk forming stereotypes.

Empathy encourages us to meet each individual as a unique person, not as a stereotype. By truly listening, we can learn about their experiences and grow beyond our assumptions.

Building Trust and Respect
If we want to live or work peacefully with people from various cultures, trust is key. Showing empathy—by asking respectful questions, listening carefully, and acknowledging different beliefs—can help build that trust. This, in turn, makes collaboration and friendship much easier.

Resolving Conflicts
Many cultural conflicts arise because people misread each other's intentions. Someone from a direct communication culture might unintentionally offend a person from a more indirect, polite culture. Empathy helps us see that neither person is wrong; they are simply following the norms they grew up with.

Encouraging Openness
Learning about other cultures can expand our own horizons. When we empathize, we become open to new ideas and traditions. Instead of seeing difference as a threat, we can see it as a chance to learn and grow.

---

3. Common Challenges in Cross-Cultural Empathy

Language Barriers
Not everyone speaks the same language, or some might not speak it fluently. Words can get lost in translation. Jokes, idioms, or slang might not make sense across languages. This can lead to misunderstandings. Even body language can mean different things in different places.

Different Communication Styles
Some cultures value directness—people say exactly what they mean. Others believe in indirect communication, using hints or polite phrases to avoid confrontation. If you come from a direct culture, you might think someone is being evasive. If you come from an indirect culture, you might find direct speech rude. This clash can block empathy if neither side tries to understand the other's style.

Time Perceptions

In some cultures, time is strict: being late is viewed as disrespectful, and schedules are closely followed. In others, events start when everyone arrives, and focusing too much on the clock can seem cold. Empathy means recognizing that neither approach is inherently right or wrong. They are just different ways to see time.

Social Hierarchies

Ideas about social roles—like how much you respect elders or how formally you address a boss—can vary widely. If you do not follow another culture's hierarchy (perhaps addressing a senior person by their first name when it is not done there), they might feel you lack respect. Understanding these rules with empathy can prevent hurt feelings.

Gestures and Body Language

Certain hand gestures that are friendly in one culture can be offensive in another. Personal space differs too. Some people stand close when talking; others need more distance. Misinterpreting these signals can lead to tension unless we try to empathize with where the other person is coming from.

---

4. Strategies to Build Cross-Cultural Empathy

1. Educate Yourself

Before interacting with people from a specific culture, do some research. This does not mean you will become an instant expert, but learning basic customs or greetings can show you care. You might look up how people greet each other or what topics might be sensitive to avoid.

2. Ask Open-Ended Questions

If you are unsure about someone's custom or point of view, politely ask. For example: "How do you usually celebrate holidays in your family?" or "What does 'on time' typically mean in your community?" Such questions show respectful curiosity, and you might learn interesting details you would never guess otherwise.

3. Listen Without Judgment

When you hear something that clashes with your own beliefs, try not to jump into saying, "That's wrong!" Instead, ask, "Could you tell me more about why that's important in your culture?" This invites deeper understanding and keeps the conversation positive.

4. Learn Some Language Basics
Even a few words—like "hello," "thank you," or "please"—in the other person's language can help build rapport. It shows you respect their culture enough to try. Do not worry about a perfect accent; the effort often matters more than perfection.

5. Watch and Observe
In a new cultural environment, pay attention to how people interact. Are they hugging, bowing, or shaking hands? Is it normal to arrive exactly on time or to come a bit later? Observing first can teach you a lot without you asking a hundred questions.

6. Share Parts of Your Culture, Too
Empathy goes both ways. Offer to tell stories or explain traditions from your own background, so the other person also feels invited to learn about you. This mutual exchange can foster a sense of equality and friendship.

---

5. Overcoming Stereotypes and Biases

Recognize Your Own Biases
We all grow up hearing certain "stories" about other groups—some might be positive, some negative, often oversimplified. Step one is being honest with yourself about these biases. Once you are aware of them, you can catch yourself thinking, "Oh, I'm slipping into a stereotype again," and instead try to see the individual in front of you.

Focus on Individuals
Whenever you meet someone from a different culture, focus on who they are as a person. Ask about their life experiences, interests, or opinions. This lessens the chance you will lump them into a broad category.

Challenge Stereotypes Openly
If a friend or family member makes a sweeping statement about a certain culture, you can gently say, "Not everyone from there is the same. Let's keep an

open mind." This can be tricky, especially if older relatives hold strong beliefs, but small reminders can help break down unhelpful generalizations.

Stay Curious
Cultural empathy is not a one-time lesson. Cultures evolve, and everyone is unique. By staying curious and learning continuously, you avoid falling into the trap of thinking you "know it all" about a group of people.

---

6. Empathy in International Travel

Research Before You Go
If you are traveling to another country, learn the basics: how to greet people, local customs, a few key phrases, proper dress codes if needed. This not only helps you avoid awkward moments but also shows respect.

Interact with Locals
Instead of sticking to tourist spots, try to meet residents. Ask for local recommendations—maybe a favorite cafe or park. People usually appreciate genuine curiosity and might share parts of their culture with you.

Embrace Mistakes
Even with the best intentions, cultural faux pas happen. You might mispronounce a word or forget to remove your shoes in a certain setting. If you make a mistake, apologize calmly and learn from it. Most people understand that newcomers are trying their best.

Be Open About Your Own Culture
Locals may also have stereotypes about visitors from your country. If they share these ideas, do not get angry. Instead, you can say, "That might be true for some people, but here's how I do it," or "In my family, we have a different tradition." This polite dialogue can bridge gaps both ways.

---

7. Cross-Cultural Empathy in the Workplace

Many modern workplaces bring together people from various cultural backgrounds. Here's how empathy can help in professional settings (building on what we discussed in Chapter 8, but from a cultural standpoint):

- **Inclusive Communication**: Encourage team members to speak up, even if English (or the main office language) is their second language. Slow down if needed, rephrase if something is unclear, and avoid too many idioms.
- **Flexible Scheduling**: If team members live in different time zones or celebrate different holidays, be mindful when planning meetings or deadlines.
- **Diversity Training**: Some companies offer workshops or training to help employees learn about cultural differences. These can be great if they focus on empathy and real-life interactions, not just dull lectures.
- **Team Building Activities**: Hosting "cultural potlucks," where everyone brings a dish from their heritage, or having short presentations about different festivals can foster empathy by letting people share parts of their lives.

---

8. Empathy in Multicultural Communities

Neighbors from Different Backgrounds
In many places, neighborhoods are home to families from all around the world. Learning a few phrases in your neighbor's language or inviting them to a community event can open doors. You might swap recipes or talk about how holidays are celebrated. These small connections can make everyone feel more at home.

Schools with Diverse Students
Teachers and parents can work together to create a caring environment for all children, regardless of cultural background. Encouraging kids to share about their traditions, celebrating multiple holidays, and avoiding negative stereotypes in classrooms can teach empathy early on.

Community Celebrations
Some towns host cultural festivals or fairs where different groups can showcase

food, music, and crafts. Attending these events—and really engaging with the people, not just sampling the food—can deepen your appreciation of diversity.

9. Balancing Cultural Empathy with Personal Boundaries

While empathy means being open and understanding, it does not mean giving up who you are. Sometimes you might disagree with a certain custom or belief. That is okay. Empathy is about seeing things from another's perspective, not necessarily adopting all their views as your own. You can respectfully share your viewpoint while honoring theirs.

There may also be times when a cultural practice clashes with your personal values to a point where you cannot support it. In such cases, you can still maintain a calm, empathetic tone, explaining where you stand without ridiculing or attacking the other person.

10. Tips for Growing Cultural Empathy

1. **Read and Watch**: Explore books, documentaries, or films from other parts of the world to get a feel for their history, art, and daily life.
2. **Attend Cultural Events**: Look for local festivals, language exchange meetups, or workshops that celebrate global traditions.
3. **Engage in Discussions**: Join community groups or online forums where people of different backgrounds share experiences. Practice listening and asking questions.
4. **Learn Another Language**: Even basic conversational skills in a new language can transform how you see the culture behind it.
5. **Reflect on Mistakes**: If a cross-cultural interaction feels awkward, reflect on it later. Did you assume something? Could you have asked a clarifying question? Use these moments as learning experiences.
6. **Stay Humble**: Recognize you will never fully grasp every nuance of another culture. That is okay. Curiosity and respect go a long way.

11. The Bigger Picture: Empathy as a Global Skill

As technology connects people from every corner of the Earth, cross-cultural empathy is more important than ever. In online discussions, we might meet people from places we have never visited, with worldviews quite different from our own. Approaching these situations with empathy can reduce online hostility and encourage meaningful exchanges.

Solving Global Issues
Challenges like climate change, global health crises, or social justice concerns often require international cooperation. Empathy allows us to see that others' problems—like a flood in a distant country—are not just "their" issues. They can also affect us in a shared global community. When we empathize, we are more likely to collaborate to find shared solutions.

Creating Friendlier Societies
On a smaller scale, but just as important, cross-cultural empathy in daily life leads to friendlier neighborhoods, less discrimination, and more inclusive workplaces. Over time, these small changes can shift our societies toward openness and kindness.

---

12. Summary

Cultural differences can sometimes feel like walls that separate people. But empathy can turn those walls into bridges. By learning about others' customs, asking respectful questions, and noticing both visible and invisible aspects of culture, we can form real connections that go beyond stereotypes.

- **Challenges**: Language barriers, different communication styles, and differing ideas about time or social hierarchy can cause misunderstandings.
- **Strategies**: Educate yourself, watch and observe, ask open-ended questions, and be ready to learn from mistakes.
- **Benefits**: Reduced prejudice, stronger trust, more effective teamwork, and a richer view of the world around us.

Cross-cultural empathy does not require giving up your own beliefs; it simply means you try to understand why others might see or do things differently. This can improve relationships in workplaces, schools, neighborhoods, and even online. As our world grows more connected, empathy serves as a vital tool that allows us to live, work, and solve problems together—despite our many differences.

In the chapters ahead, we will further explore the role of empathy in **digital communication** and **self-awareness**, continuing to build on everything we have covered so far. Each new setting offers its own challenges and rewards, but the core idea remains the same: by seeing other people as real human beings with genuine feelings and experiences, we make the world just a bit more caring, compassionate, and united.

Chapter 11: Digital Communication and Empathy

We live in an age where digital communication is everywhere. We send messages, share updates, and express ourselves on social media, email, and instant messaging apps. We connect with friends, family, coworkers, and even strangers from around the world—all with a few taps on a screen. As wonderful as this is, it also creates new challenges for empathy. When we cannot see someone's face, hear their voice, or sense their body language, it becomes harder to fully grasp their feelings. And just as importantly, it becomes easier to forget that there is a real human on the other end of our device.

In this chapter, we will explore how empathy can thrive—or fail—in digital spaces. We will talk about common communication pitfalls online, ways to show understanding despite the lack of face-to-face contact, and strategies to keep empathy alive on social media, in emails, and beyond. By the end, you will have fresh ideas on how to bring empathy into every corner of your digital life.

---

1. Why Empathy Often Suffers in Digital Communication

Lack of Visual Cues
In a face-to-face conversation, you can see a person's expression, posture, or gestures. This helps you notice if they are sad, offended, or excited. But online, you only see words on a screen—maybe a profile picture, but not always. Without visual cues, it is easy to misunderstand someone's tone or intention.

Delayed or Short Responses
Many digital chats happen in quick bursts. Sometimes people respond hours later, or they reply with very short messages like "K" or "Fine." This can leave you guessing how they really feel. A short "Okay" might mean they are busy or upset or just uninterested. Because you do not have a lot of context, you might assume the worst.

Anonymity and "Keyboard Courage"
When people communicate behind screens, some feel emboldened to say harsh things they would never say in person. They might leave insulting comments or

engage in bullying. This can happen because they do not see the immediate hurt on someone's face, so they do not feel the emotional impact of their words. This kind of behavior can weaken empathy.

Fear of Missing Out (FOMO)
Social media often shows only the highlights of people's lives—happy moments, achievements, vacations. This can cause jealousy, sadness, or insecurity for those who feel left out. It also can create an environment where we do not fully empathize with each other's real struggles, because everyone seems to be doing fine on the surface.

---

2. The Power of Empathy in Digital Spaces

Despite these hurdles, empathy can still flourish online. Many people form lasting friendships or even find support groups on the internet. In fact, digital communication can sometimes make empathy more accessible for shy or introverted people, who find it easier to open up in writing.

Support Networks
There are online communities for just about any issue—mental health challenges, parenting questions, chronic illnesses, or hobby interests. In these spaces, people often share personal stories and offer each other emotional backing. Empathy is the glue that holds these groups together.

Global Perspective
Through social media or international forums, we can hear from people living in vastly different cultures or life situations. This can open our eyes to struggles or joys we did not know existed. The more we learn about one another, the easier it can be to empathize across cultural lines.

Convenient Communication
Digital channels let us connect with someone even if we are miles apart. We can quickly send a supportive message when they are having a tough day, or share in their happiness when they get good news. Empathy does not have to wait for an in-person meeting—it can happen anytime, anywhere.

---

3. Empathetic Communication on Social Media

Social media apps like Facebook, Instagram, Twitter, TikTok, and others are a huge part of everyday life for many people. While these platforms can be fun and informative, they also come with challenges to empathy.

1. Slow Down Before You Comment
It is easy to dash off a quick reply, especially if you disagree with something. But a hasty comment might sound rude or hurtful. Take a moment to consider how your words might land. If you were in their shoes, how would you feel reading your comment?

2. Think About Context
Sometimes, people post things when they are emotional—angry, sad, or stressed. If you see a friend sharing a strong opinion or venting, try to understand that there might be deeper feelings behind their words. Ask gentle questions to clarify: "Are you okay? You sound upset."

3. Engage in Constructive Dialogue
If you see a post you disagree with, you can respond empathetically. Instead of saying, "That's stupid!" you could say, "I have a different viewpoint. Can you tell me more about why you believe that?" This opens a space for conversation and respect.

4. Avoid Public Fights
When people argue publicly in the comments section, it can escalate fast, with others jumping in and making it worse. If you see an issue worth discussing, consider taking it to a private message or DM. This can keep the talk more respectful.

5. Use Emojis or Tones Wisely
Words can sound cold without context. Simple additions—like saying "I'm happy for you!" with a smiley face—can convey warmth. But be careful not to rely on emojis alone if the topic is serious. Saying, "I'm sorry for your loss \uD83D\uDE22" might seem less genuine than a thoughtful sentence or two.

4. Being Mindful in Text and Instant Messaging

Whether it is with friends, family, or coworkers, text and instant messaging apps (like WhatsApp, Messenger, Slack, or Discord) are key tools in daily communication. Here's how to keep empathy in mind:

Check the Tone
Text messages do not always carry tone well. A quick "I need to talk to you" can sound scary or harsh. Adding a softener like, "Hey, when you have a moment, could we chat? Nothing urgent" can reduce anxiety for the receiver.

Reply with Care
If you sense the person is upset or stressed, take a moment to offer empathy. Even a short note like, "I'm sorry you're going through this. Let me know if you want to talk more," can make a big difference.

Use Active Listening
Yes, you can use active listening over text. For example, if a friend vents about a bad day, you might respond, "So you're feeling frustrated because your boss gave you extra work without warning, right?" This shows you truly heard them.

Timing Matters
We all have different schedules. Be mindful of when you text. Sending a flurry of messages late at night might disturb someone's rest, especially if the topic is heavy. If it is urgent, it might be better to call, so they know it is important.

---

5. Empathy in Email and Professional Settings

Workplaces and formal contexts rely heavily on email. Many of us have experienced confusion or conflict because an email's tone was misunderstood. Here is how to keep empathy in professional emails:

Use a Friendly Greeting
"Hello [Name], I hope you're doing well," can set a courteous tone before you dive into the main point. It costs nothing to be polite.

Be Clear and Respectful
Sometimes, people can sound bossy or rude if they are not careful with words.

Avoid phrases like "You must do this now." Instead, try "Could we have this done by Thursday?" or "Let's aim for Thursday—does that work for you?" This respects the other person's perspective.

Address Problems Calmly
If you have to point out a mistake, do it with empathy. For example, "I noticed an error in the report. Let's work together to fix it," sounds more supportive than "You messed up the report."

Recognize Cultural Differences
Email etiquette varies across cultures. Some places expect very direct language; others see that as impolite. If you are emailing people from different countries, consider the possibility that their style might differ from yours. Be patient and kind.

---

6. Handling Online Criticism or Hostility with Empathy

Stay Calm
When someone attacks you or leaves a nasty comment, your first reaction might be anger. Try to pause and cool down before responding. Sometimes, ignoring a troll (someone who posts just to provoke others) is the best approach. If the conflict is genuine, a calm, empathetic reply can defuse it.

Acknowledge Their Feelings
If someone is upset with you, see if you can find a nugget of truth in what they say. For example, "I hear that you're frustrated because you feel I didn't credit your contribution. I'm sorry you feel that way." Even if you do not fully agree, showing you hear them can soften the tension.

Offer a Path Forward
Empathy does not mean you have to accept abuse or agree with everything said. But you can propose a solution or next step. "Let's talk more in private messages and see if we can sort this out," or "I'd like to understand your point of view better. Can we chat offline?"

Protect Your Well-Being
If the person is being abusive or threatening, empathy for yourself matters. It is

okay to block them or report the behavior on social platforms. Your safety and mental health come first.

---

7. Group Chats, Forums, and Online Communities

Rules and Moderation
Many online groups have moderators who set rules. These rules (such as "no hate speech" or "no personal attacks") try to keep the environment respectful. Following these guidelines is part of showing empathy for the group's well-being.

Give More Than You Take
If you join a group where people help each other (like a coding forum or a parenting group), do not just show up, ask a question, and leave. Offer help or share your own experiences too. This builds a spirit of mutual support.

Encourage Those Who Are Struggling
Sometimes, people post about their problems hoping for empathy. Even if you are not an expert, a kind word like, "I'm sorry you're dealing with this," or "I hope things get better soon," can provide comfort. You do not have to solve their problem to show you care.

Respect Privacy
In group settings, be careful about sharing private messages or personal info. What someone shares in a closed group might be sensitive. Ask permission if you want to share their story elsewhere, or keep their details vague to protect them.

---

8. Digital Self-Awareness to Support Empathy

Notice Your Mood Before Posting
If you are stressed, angry, or tired, you may write something harsher than you mean. Consider waiting before replying, or drafting a response and reading it again later when you are calmer.

Watch for Confirmation Bias
Online platforms often show us content that matches our interests or beliefs. This can create an "echo chamber," where we see only opinions similar to ours.

Try to step outside your bubble sometimes. Follow diverse voices or read opposing views—empathetically.

Limit Screen Time
Being glued to social media can lead to burnout or impulsive replies. Setting boundaries—like not checking email late at night or limiting social media scrolling—can help you stay mentally healthy. A healthier mind supports better empathy.

Reflect on Your Online Interactions
After a heated discussion or a supportive exchange, take a moment to think: "Did I respond with empathy? Could I have been kinder? Did I truly understand the other person's side?" Over time, this habit helps you grow more empathetic online.

---

9. Teaching Kids and Teens Empathy Online

Many kids have smartphones and are active on social media from an early age. They need guidance to develop digital empathy.

Explain the Human Factor
Remind them that behind each profile is a real person with feelings. If they receive or witness mean comments, discuss how that might affect someone. Encourage them to show kindness online, just like in person.

Set Communication Guidelines
Talk about what is okay to post and what is not. For example, never share someone else's embarrassing photo without permission. Show them how to block or report bullies if necessary.

Practice Together
Look at a friend's post and ask, "How do you think they feel?" or "What would a caring response look like?" This teaches them to think about empathy before they type.

Monitor Gently
Depending on their age, you might keep an eye on what they do online. Not to

spy, but to ensure they are treating others respectfully and learning from any mistakes.

10. Balancing Authenticity and Privacy

Being Genuine
Empathy often grows when we share genuine parts of ourselves. However, online spaces can be risky for oversharing personal details (like addresses or deep family secrets). Finding a balance—being honest but also safe—is key.

Establish Boundaries
You decide how much you want to reveal about your life. If someone pushes you to share more than you are comfortable with, it is okay to politely decline. Empathy does not require revealing everything about yourself.

Honoring Others' Boundaries
Just as you have limits, others do too. If a friend does not want to discuss a certain topic online, respect that. Pushing them can harm trust and reduce empathy.

11. Future Trends: Empathy and Technology

Virtual Reality (VR) and Empathy
Some people think VR might create deeper empathy by letting us "see" the world through someone else's eyes. For example, VR experiences can show what it is like to live with a disability or be in a war zone. This can be powerful, but it is still developing.

Artificial Intelligence (AI)
AI chatbots can mimic human conversation. While they might give quick answers or comfort, real empathy needs a human element. Still, AI might help people who are lonely or need mental health resources, especially if no human is available at the moment. We must keep a balance between helpful technology and genuine human connection.

Privacy and Ethics

As technology grows, issues of data privacy become bigger. Empathy means we should care about how personal info is used or shared. Encouraging companies to handle data responsibly is part of caring about each other's well-being.

12. Summary

Digital communication can either block empathy or help it grow—much depends on our choices. When we remember that real people lie behind usernames, we can respond with thoughtfulness and respect. Slowing down before commenting, asking clarifying questions, and showing genuine concern all lead to more empathetic interactions.

- **Challenges**: Lack of face-to-face cues, short or delayed messages, anonymity leading to harsh words, and social media pressure can weaken empathy.
- **Opportunities**: Online support groups, global connections, and quick communication can spread understanding quickly if used wisely.
- **Practical Tips**: Be mindful of tone, use a friendly approach in emails, manage your mood before posting, and seek constructive dialogue rather than fights.

By using empathy on social media, in texts, emails, and any digital platform, we show that technology does not have to divide us—it can bring us closer. In the next chapter, we will move from the digital world to a more personal realm: how **building self-awareness** can boost our empathy skills in all areas of life. Being aware of our own feelings and triggers is often the first step to truly understanding others.

Chapter 12: Building Self-Awareness to Improve Empathy

Empathy is not just about looking outward—feeling what someone else feels. It also involves looking inward to understand our own emotions, thoughts, and triggers. **Self-awareness** is the practice of noticing what is happening in your own mind and heart at any moment. When you are more self-aware, you can handle your emotions in a healthy way, respond thoughtfully instead of reacting blindly, and make room for the feelings of others. In short, self-awareness strengthens your ability to empathize.

In this chapter, we will talk about the link between self-awareness and empathy, explore practices to become more aware of your own inner world, and discuss how this deeper understanding of yourself can lead to richer, kinder connections with others.

---

1. The Connection Between Self-Awareness and Empathy

Knowing Your Own Emotions First
If you are not in touch with your own feelings, it is harder to understand what someone else might be going through. For instance, if you are feeling frustrated but do not realize it, you might become impatient or snap at a friend who is venting. On the other hand, if you know you are frustrated, you can say, "I'm a bit stressed today. Let me take a breath before I respond," which keeps the conversation calmer and more empathetic.

Controlling Biases
We all have biases—preferences, dislikes, past hurts—that color how we see other people. Self-awareness helps you notice these biases. For example, if you realize you have a bias against people who speak very loudly, you can catch yourself before you unfairly judge someone who has a loud voice. Recognizing your bias frees you to hear their message without dismissing them.

Greater Emotional Resilience
Self-awareness is like a muscle that helps you handle strong emotions without letting them rule you. When you can handle your own feelings, you are less likely

to become defensive or overwhelmed by someone else's feelings. This makes empathy more stable and genuine.

Choosing Thoughtful Responses
Empathy requires slowing down to connect with what the other person feels. Self-awareness gives you a mental "pause button." Instead of reacting instantly, you can notice, "I feel annoyed," or "I feel worried," and then choose a response that reflects compassion rather than raw emotion.

---

2. Signs You Might Lack Self-Awareness

Frequent Conflicts
If you often find yourself in arguments, it could be a sign that you are not noticing your triggers. You might be lashing out without understanding your own emotional state first.

Difficulty Processing Emotions
Maybe you are quick to anger but are not sure why. Or you feel sadness but cannot trace where it is coming from. Lacking self-awareness can leave you confused about your own feelings.

Blaming Others for Everything
People who are low on self-awareness might blame everyone else for misunderstandings or fights. They do not see how their own behavior might contribute to problems.

Feeling Disconnected from Your Inner World
If you rarely reflect on your feelings, goals, or values, you might have a weak sense of self-awareness. Life might feel like it is on autopilot.

---

3. Pathways to Greater Self-Awareness

The good news is that self-awareness is a skill you can develop over time. Here are some tried-and-true methods:

1. Mindful Breathing
Taking a few minutes each day to focus on your breath can ground you in the present moment. Sit quietly, close your eyes if comfortable, and notice the air entering and leaving your nostrils. If your mind wanders, gently bring it back to your breath. This practice helps you become aware of your mental chatter and emotional undercurrents.

2. Journaling
Writing down your thoughts and feelings can reveal patterns you did not notice. You could write about your day, something that upset you, or a moment of gratitude. Over time, you may see triggers that spark strong emotions or realize what truly brings you joy.

3. Regular Check-Ins
Pause throughout the day—maybe set an alarm on your phone—and ask yourself, "How do I feel right now?" Give a name to the emotion (like sad, happy, anxious, bored). This simple labeling process helps you recognize moods before they take over.

4. Meditation or Yoga
Meditation, beyond just breathing, can teach you to observe thoughts and emotions without judgment. Yoga integrates body awareness, teaching you to notice tension, posture, and breath. Both can boost your sense of being "in tune" with yourself.

5. Therapy or Counseling
Talking with a therapist can offer professional insight into your inner world. A counselor might help you unpack past experiences that shape your current reactions. Therapy is not just for major problems; it can be a tool for personal growth and self-awareness.

---

4. Common Emotional Triggers and How to Spot Them

History of Hurt
If you were teased in childhood about something—your appearance, for instance—comments about it now might trigger anger or insecurity. Self-awareness means noticing that jump in your emotions and connecting it to past pain.

Fear of Failure
Some people react strongly when they feel they have messed up. They might lash out or blame others. Recognizing that fear of failure is your trigger can help you respond more calmly.

Feeling Unheard or Disrespected
If you have had experiences where your voice was ignored, even small signs of dismissal can set you off. Self-awareness helps you see this pattern and address it with empathy (for yourself and for the other person).

Comparisons
Comparing yourself to others can spark envy or shame. If you catch yourself feeling stressed after seeing someone's "perfect life" online, that is a sign you are triggered by comparisons. With self-awareness, you can remind yourself that social media is rarely the full story.

---

5. Linking Self-Awareness to Empathy in Daily Life

Handling Conflict Gracefully
When a disagreement arises, self-awareness helps you notice if your frustration is mostly about the current issue or something else (like being tired or anxious about unrelated matters). You might realize, "I'm snapping at my partner because I'm worried about work tomorrow, not because they actually did anything terrible." This insight can calm you down and allow you to empathize better with them.

Showing Understanding Instead of Reacting
Maybe a coworker is being short-tempered. Self-awareness can reveal you are feeling defensive. But instead of firing back, you might choose empathy: "They might be under pressure today. Let me ask if they are okay or if they need help."

Listening More Deeply
When you know your own emotional habits, it is easier to set them aside temporarily and focus on the other person. If you tend to interrupt when anxious, self-awareness lets you catch yourself and say, "Hold on, let me let them finish."

Giving Others Space
Sometimes, people want to share something heavy or personal. If you are aware you are emotionally drained or triggered, you can kindly say, "I want to give you my full attention, but can we talk in about 30 minutes so I can clear my head?" You are respecting your own limits and also ensuring you can truly be there for them.

---

6. Self-Compassion as a Path to Empathy

Self-awareness should not turn into self-criticism. If you find something in yourself that you do not like—maybe anger flares or jealousy—be kind to yourself. Acknowledge that you are human and that we all have flaws. This is **self-compassion**, and it is closely tied to empathy for others.

Why Self-Compassion Helps
If you beat yourself up for your mistakes, you might become defensive when others make mistakes, too. On the other hand, if you treat your own failings with kindness, you are more likely to treat others with kindness when they fail. It is a simple concept: how you speak to yourself shapes how you speak to the world.

Practicing Self-Compassion
When you notice a fault or a painful feeling, try saying, "This is hard. It's okay to feel upset. I'm doing my best." This does not excuse bad behavior, but it also does not shame you. With gentleness toward yourself, you free up energy to empathize with others.

---

7. Tools and Exercises for Deeper Self-Awareness

Emotion Wheel
Some people use an "emotion wheel," a circle chart with basic emotions in the center (like sad, angry, happy, scared) branching out into more specific feelings (bored, irritated, nostalgic, anxious). When you feel something, look at the wheel to identify the closest match. This can expand your emotional vocabulary.

Morning Pages
This idea, popularized by an author named Julia Cameron, is to write three pages

of anything each morning. It is a brain dump—no editing or worrying about grammar. By doing this consistently, you might uncover hidden worries, hopes, or ideas that you can then address.

"HALT" Check
"HALT" stands for Hungry, Angry, Lonely, Tired. These four states often cause us to lose our cool or empathy. Before reacting strongly, ask yourself, "Am I hungry, angry, lonely, or tired?" If so, address that need first—eat, rest, talk to a friend—before dealing with the situation.

Mindful Walks
Take a short walk without listening to music or looking at your phone. Focus on the sights and sounds around you. Notice how your body feels with each step. If your mind drifts to worries, gently bring it back to the present moment. This can calm you and sharpen your self-awareness.

---

8. Managing Overwhelm and Stress

Sometimes, life gets so busy or stressful that self-awareness slips. We operate on autopilot, just trying to get through the day. That can make empathy vanish. We snap at people or ignore their feelings because we are drained.

Set Realistic Goals
Overcommitment can lead to constant stress. Learn to say "no" when you cannot handle extra tasks. This keeps your mind clearer and your empathy tank fuller.

Plan for Downtime
Try scheduling small breaks in the day—time for a short walk, a snack, or a moment to breathe. Just five minutes of quiet can reset your emotional balance.

Use Stress as a Signal
When you feel stressed, do not just power through mindlessly. Check in with yourself: "Why am I stressed? Is there something I can change or ask for help with?" Identifying the source can keep stress from controlling you.

Release Tension Physically
Some people benefit from exercise, stretching, or even just shaking out their

arms and legs to relieve tension. This physical release can help your mind settle, too.

---

9. Helping Others Develop Self-Awareness

If you are leading a team, raising kids, or just caring for loved ones, you might want to encourage them to be more self-aware. Here are some gentle ways:

Lead by Example
Show them how you manage your emotions. If you get upset, you might say out loud, "I'm feeling a bit angry right now, so I'm going to take a quick walk to calm down." They see a real-life example of emotional regulation.

Ask Questions
If a friend is venting, you can ask, "How do you feel about this?" or "What do you think is causing that feeling?" This nudges them to look inward.

Recommend Helpful Tools
Share a journaling app, a guided meditation, or a book about self-awareness. Offer them, but do not force them. Everyone grows at their own pace.

Practice Active Listening
When someone tries to open up about their emotions, listen without judgment. Reflect back what they say so they feel heard. This supportive space can inspire them to explore their feelings further.

---

10. Balancing Self-Awareness with Others' Needs

There is a sweet spot in empathy: you respect your own feelings while also caring about others. It is not always easy. Some people focus so much on themselves that they ignore others' needs (selfishness), while others sacrifice themselves entirely to please others (self-abandonment).

Healthy Boundaries
A boundary is a line that protects your well-being. For example, if you know you get overwhelmed by too many social events, you might limit yourself to one

outing per weekend. That way, you stay emotionally healthy enough to be empathetic when you do see people.

Check Your Motives
Are you being overly kind just to avoid conflict, even if it hurts you? That might lead to resentment. Or are you ignoring someone else's feelings because you do not want to deal with them? Self-awareness means noticing these patterns and adjusting toward healthy empathy.

Communicate Openly
Tell people how you feel. If you need to rest or cannot take on another project, be honest. Often, others appreciate the clarity and might even show empathy back.

---

11. Growth Over Time

Building self-awareness is not a quick fix; it is a lifelong practice. You will have days of great clarity and days when you feel lost. That is normal. The important thing is to keep making small efforts—journaling, meditating, reflecting after emotional incidents. Over the months and years, you will likely notice:

- **Less Reactive Behavior**: You snap or yell less often.
- **Improved Relationships**: People sense you are calmer and more genuinely interested in them.
- **Greater Confidence**: Knowing yourself well can help you stand up for your needs and beliefs.
- **Deepened Empathy**: Since you understand your own inner workings, you can better relate to others' struggles and joys.

---

12. Summary

Self-awareness is the foundation upon which empathy stands. By paying attention to your own feelings, biases, and triggers, you become better equipped to tune in to someone else's experience. Self-awareness practices—like mindful breathing, journaling, and regular emotional check-ins—help you handle stress, make kinder choices, and stay present for the people in your life.

- **Why It Matters**: Without self-awareness, empathy can become shallow or vanish under stress.
- **Key Strategies**: Mindfulness, journaling, checking for emotional triggers, and setting healthy boundaries all boost self-awareness.
- **Impact**: As you grow more aware, your empathy for others naturally deepens. You become more patient, understanding, and supportive in personal and professional relationships.

In the next chapter, we will take a closer look at **healing emotional wounds through empathy**—both for yourself and for others. Wounds from the past can linger, coloring how we relate to people. Empathy, combined with strong self-awareness, can be a healing force that helps us move forward with less fear and more openness.

Chapter 13: Healing Emotional Wounds Through Empathy

Emotional wounds are hurts that go deeper than physical injuries. They can come from past trauma, heartbreak, betrayal, or loss. While cuts and scrapes on the body might heal in days or weeks, emotional wounds can linger for years, shaping how we see the world and how we relate to ourselves and others. These hidden hurts can make it difficult to trust or open up. They can keep us feeling stuck in anger, shame, or sadness. Fortunately, **empathy** can help us heal.

Empathy allows us to feel truly heard and understood, which is often what our wounded hearts need. This chapter explores how emotional wounds form, how empathy can help us heal them, and the practical ways to invite empathy into our journey toward recovery. Whether you are dealing with your own past hurts or supporting someone else, empathy can be a powerful bridge from pain toward hope.

---

1. Understanding Emotional Wounds

Where Do Emotional Wounds Come From?

- **Trauma**: Events like abuse, violence, accidents, or sudden loss can scar us emotionally.
- **Betrayal**: When someone we trust breaks that trust, the sense of hurt can run very deep.
- **Rejection**: Being left out, bullied, or turned down can plant seeds of shame or unworthiness.
- **Chronic Stress**: Sometimes it is not one big event, but a string of smaller stresses or criticisms that chip away at our sense of security.

Why Do They Last So Long?
Emotional wounds linger because they shape how we interpret new experiences. If you were repeatedly criticized as a child, you might hear mild feedback at work as a harsh attack. This constant reminder of old pain means the wound never fully closes unless you actively address it.

Signs of an Unhealed Emotional Wound

- You feel an intense reaction to a small trigger (like panic, deep sadness, or anger).
- You avoid certain situations or people for fear of being hurt again.
- You sense a loss of trust—either in yourself or in others.
- You carry guilt or shame you cannot explain logically.
- You find it tough to form close bonds, because you expect to be hurt or let down.

---

2. The Role of Empathy in Healing

Safe Space to Share
One of the first steps in healing is being able to express your pain. Empathy, either from a trusted friend, therapist, or support group, gives you a safe space to share your story. When someone listens without judgment, you feel less alone.

Validation
Emotional wounds can cause doubts about whether your feelings are "valid." An empathetic listener can say, "It makes sense that you feel this way," or "I see how this hurt you." Hearing that your experience is real and worthy of attention can ease some of the burden.

Reconnecting with Feelings
Sometimes, when we have been hurt, we numb ourselves or block out emotions so we do not have to feel pain again. But healing often requires gently reconnecting with those feelings. Empathy helps by making that process safer. When we know someone cares, we may be more willing to explore the hurt, grief, or fear.

Developing Self-Compassion
Empathy from others can also teach us to be kinder to ourselves. If others treat our pain with tenderness, we begin to see that we, too, can show kindness to our own wounds. Over time, this self-compassion speeds healing by reducing self-blame and shame.

---

3. Empathy for Yourself: Self-Empathy

Why Self-Empathy Matters
While receiving empathy from others is important, self-empathy is the ongoing practice of turning compassion inward. After all, we are with ourselves 24/7. If our own internal voice is harsh or dismissive, healing can only go so far. Self-empathy means speaking to yourself with the same warmth you would offer a dear friend.

Practicing Self-Empathy

1. **Acknowledge the Pain**: Instead of pushing negative feelings away, notice them. "I am feeling sadness right now. It's okay to feel this."
2. **Offer Understanding**: Remind yourself why this feeling makes sense. "Of course I'm sad—I lost something important."
3. **Provide Comfort**: It might be a calm statement like, "I'm here for you," or a soothing action, like taking a warm bath or cuddling with a pet.
4. **Release Judgment**: Try not to label your emotions as "good" or "bad." They are signals, not moral failures.

Self-Empathy vs. Self-Pity
Self-empathy is not about wallowing in sorrow or thinking, "Poor me, everything is hopeless." It is about recognizing pain, offering kindness, and then deciding how to respond. Sometimes that response is seeking professional help, journaling, or talking to a friend. Other times, it might be setting new boundaries or making a healthy change in your life.

---

4. Giving Empathy to Someone with Emotional Wounds

1. Listen Without Fixing
When a loved one shares their pain, resist the urge to jump in with quick solutions or advice—unless they specifically ask for it. Often, what they need most is for someone to listen and say, "I hear you. That sounds hard." Being listened to with care can already be a big step toward healing.

2. Validate Their Feelings
Let them know it is okay to feel hurt, angry, or confused. You can say, "I can see why that would make you upset," or "It sounds like you have been carrying this

for a long time." Validating does not mean you agree with every detail, but you acknowledge their emotional reality.

3. Offer Help Gently
Sometimes, people with deep wounds may not know what help is available, like counseling, support groups, or simply talking more regularly. You can offer: "I'm here if you want to explore therapy options," or "Would you like me to check in more often?" But leave the choice up to them.

4. Be Patient
Healing emotional wounds is not a fast process. It can take weeks, months, or even years to fully recover, especially if the trauma is severe. You might notice them making progress, then having setbacks. Patience and steady empathy can help them trust the healing process.

---

5. Exploring Healing Methods That Involve Empathy

Therapy and Counseling
Many forms of therapy rely on empathy as a core element. Therapists offer a nonjudgmental space for clients to express painful memories. Techniques such as Cognitive Behavioral Therapy (CBT) or Eye Movement Desensitization and Reprocessing (EMDR) can help reframe traumatic events, but the therapist's empathetic presence is often what makes clients feel safe enough to process those events.

Support Groups
Groups for grief, addiction recovery, or trauma survivors are built on shared empathy. Members relate to each other's stories, reducing the sense of isolation. Hearing "I've been there too" can be a profound relief.

Art and Music
Creative activities can bring emotional wounds to the surface in a gentle way. When done in a group or with a supportive friend, empathy can flow as people share their drawings, songs, or poems about their experiences. Even without words, there is understanding.

Mindfulness Programs
Practices like mindfulness-based stress reduction teach participants to be kind

observers of their own feelings and thoughts. In group settings, participants often share their journeys, providing empathy to each other's struggles with stress, anxiety, or sadness.

---

6. Overcoming Resistance to Empathy

Sometimes, people with deep hurts resist empathy. They might say, "You couldn't possibly understand," or "I don't need anyone's pity." This reaction can come from fear of being vulnerable or from past disappointments where they reached out and got hurt again. How can we gently work through this barrier?

Build Trust Step by Step
If someone is closed off, start with small gestures: a kind word, a genuine "How are you?" Don't push them to open up right away. Let them set the pace.

Respect Their Boundaries
If they say they do not want to talk about it, forcing them can backfire. You can let them know you are available if they change their mind. That sense of choice can keep the door open for the future.

Show Consistency
If you promise to be there, keep your word. Emotional wounds often involve broken trust, so consistently showing up can rebuild a sense of safety.

Acknowledge Their Fears
You might say, "I know it's scary to trust again, especially if you've been hurt before. I won't judge you or push you. I just want you to know I care."

---

7. Specific Scenarios Where Empathy Aids Healing

Heartbreak from a Relationship Ending
Breakups can leave people feeling abandoned or unworthy. Empathy—whether from friends or family—can remind the wounded person that they are still lovable and valuable. Simple supportive gestures like offering to listen, sending them a thoughtful text, or inviting them for a walk can help them feel less isolated.

Loss of a Loved One
Grief is one of the deepest pains. Empathy in the form of listening to memories, acknowledging the depth of the loss, and avoiding clichés ("They're in a better place") can bring comfort. Sometimes, just sitting quietly with someone who is crying can be an act of profound empathy.

Workplace Trauma
We do not always consider the emotional harm that can happen at work—bullying, being fired unfairly, or facing discrimination. Empathy from colleagues, a mentor, or a counselor can prevent long-term damage to the person's self-esteem and sense of safety. Recognizing they were treated poorly and encouraging them to seek help (legal advice if needed, or therapy) can start the healing process.

Childhood Abuse
Abuse that happens early in life can shape a person's entire worldview, making them believe the world is unsafe or that they are somehow to blame. Therapists, support groups, or close friends who offer empathy (rather than judgment or disbelief) can help survivors piece together a healthier self-image and trust in humanity again.

---

8. Balancing Empathy and Personal Boundaries

When you are supporting someone with emotional wounds, it is easy to get pulled into their pain. While empathy is crucial, you also need to maintain your own emotional health. If you do not, you risk **empathy burnout**, where you become exhausted or numb from carrying another's pain. Some tips for keeping a healthy balance:

- **Recognize Your Limits**: Be honest about how much time or emotional energy you can give.
- **Encourage Professional Help**: If their trauma is severe, gently suggest they see a counselor.
- **Self-Care**: Make sure you have your own support system and healthy outlets for stress.
- **Set Boundaries Kindly**: You can say, "I want to support you, but I need to rest tonight. Let's talk tomorrow."

9. Celebrating Small Steps in Healing

Healing emotional wounds is not typically about one grand breakthrough. It is often a journey made of small, meaningful steps—like being able to talk about a painful event without crying, or trusting someone enough to share a secret, or simply feeling a little lighter after months of heaviness. Recognizing these small wins can fuel hope.

You might keep a journal of progress:

- "Today, I talked about my past without shutting down."
- "I let a friend hug me when I was sad, and it felt okay."
- "I noticed I didn't panic when someone raised their voice at work."

Each small step shows that healing is possible and that empathy—both from yourself and from others—is working.

10. The Ongoing Nature of Healing

Some emotional wounds do heal fully, where we no longer feel pain or sadness about that event. Others may leave a "scar," meaning we can function well and live a good life, but we still have some tenderness when we recall what happened. That is normal. Healing is not about erasing the past but learning to live with it in a healthier way.

Empathy helps us see that pain does not isolate us. Our experiences—whether heartbreak, loss, or betrayal—are shared by countless others. By connecting with people who understand or empathize, we find the strength to move forward. Empathy reminds us we are never truly alone, even in our darkest moments.

11. Summary

Emotional wounds are deep hurts that can shape our sense of self and color how we see others. They arise from trauma, loss, betrayal, or extended stress, and they do not heal on their own with time. **Empathy**—from friends, professionals, support groups, and ourselves—is a vital ingredient in that healing process. It offers a safe space to share pain, validates our feelings, and helps us reconnect with our emotions in a healthier way.

- **Self-Empathy**: Being kind to ourselves, acknowledging our hurt, and speaking gently to our inner wounds.
- **Supportive Empathy from Others**: Listening without trying to fix, validating emotions, and offering gentle help when asked.
- **Healing Methods**: Therapy, group support, artistic expression, and mindfulness all use empathy as a foundation to help people process and move beyond old hurts.
- **Moving Forward**: While emotional scars may remain, empathy builds understanding, resilience, and hope. Each small step in healing is worth celebrating.

In the next chapter, we will explore how to balance empathy with the need for **healthy boundaries**. It is possible to care deeply for others without losing yourself or running out of emotional energy. Understanding boundaries helps us maintain a stable, nurturing environment for ourselves and the people we empathize with.

Chapter 14: Setting Healthy Boundaries While Being Empathetic

Empathy is a wonderful trait—understanding and caring about people's feelings helps us form deeper connections. But sometimes, we might overextend ourselves and lose track of our own limits. That is where **boundaries** come in. Boundaries are the guidelines or rules we set to protect our well-being, energy, and mental health. They help us decide how we spend our time, who we share our personal space with, and how we engage emotionally with others.

In this chapter, we will discuss why boundaries are essential, how to set them without shutting down empathy, and ways to respect other people's boundaries as well. By the end, you will see that it is possible to show compassion while also caring for your own emotional needs. These two are not at odds; they actually support each other. When we have strong boundaries, our empathy is more sustainable, honest, and helpful.

---

1. What Are Boundaries and Why Do They Matter?

Boundaries Defined
Boundaries are the limits or lines you draw around your personal space, emotions, and time. They say, "This is okay with me, that is not." They do not have to be rigid walls; they can be flexible, but they must be clear enough to protect your peace.

Common Types of Boundaries

1. **Physical Boundaries**: Who can touch you, how close they can stand, or when you need personal space.
2. **Emotional Boundaries**: Deciding what emotional burdens you can handle, how much you can listen to someone's problems, and what topics you feel safe discussing.
3. **Time Boundaries**: How much of your day you can give to others' requests. If you are constantly taking on extra tasks or social invites, you might need a boundary here.

4. **Mental Boundaries**: The ideas or beliefs you hold dear, and how you handle disagreements.
5. **Material Boundaries**: How you share or lend your things—money, car, or personal belongings.

Why Boundaries Are Important

- They prevent burnout.
- They protect you from being taken advantage of.
- They give you room to recharge, so you can offer empathy in a healthy way.
- They reduce resentment, because you are clear about what you can and cannot do.

---

2. Misconceptions About Boundaries and Empathy

Myth 1: Boundaries Mean You Are Cold
Some people think saying "no" is mean or selfish. In reality, saying "yes" to everything can cause exhaustion or half-hearted help. It is kinder to give genuine assistance when you can, rather than forced help every time.

Myth 2: Empathy Means Having No Limits
Empathy does not require you to absorb everyone's problems until you have none of your own space left. You can understand someone's struggles while still recognizing, "I am not able to solve all their issues," or "I need time to myself now."

Myth 3: Strong Boundaries Drive People Away
Actually, healthy boundaries often improve relationships. By being clear, you prevent misunderstandings. The people who truly care about you usually respect your limits and appreciate that you are honest about them.

---

3. Signs You Might Need Stronger Boundaries

1. **You Feel Constantly Drained**: If every conversation leaves you exhausted, you might be giving too much emotional energy without refilling your own cup.
2. **Frequent Resentment**: Do you feel annoyed or bitter when people ask for your help? This is often a clue that you are saying "yes" too often or not communicating your needs.
3. **Difficulty Saying 'No'**: If guilt swamps you whenever you want to say "no," you might be ignoring your own limits.
4. **Blurred Personal Space**: Maybe people show up unannounced at your home, or call you at all hours, and you feel you cannot push back.
5. **Over-Involvement in Others' Problems**: If someone has a problem, do you immediately feel responsible for fixing it? This might mean your empathy has turned into boundaryless caretaking.

---

4. How to Set Boundaries Without Losing Empathy

Step 1: Identify Your Needs
Reflect on times you felt overwhelmed or taken advantage of. Ask yourself, "Which area (time, emotional, physical, etc.) is being breached?" Knowing your needs is the first step to protecting them.

Step 2: Communicate Clearly
You can be polite and firm at the same time. For example, if a friend always calls late at night, you might say, "I care about you, but I need my rest. Could we talk earlier in the evening instead?" Notice how you express empathy ("I care about you") while also setting a limit ("I need my rest").

Step 3: Propose Alternatives
Sometimes, you cannot give someone what they want, but you can offer another option. If a coworker wants your help with a project and you have no time, you might say, "I can't do extra tasks this week, but maybe next Tuesday I can give you an hour, or you could check with [another colleague] who knows about this."

Step 4: Stick to It
Setting a boundary is one thing; maintaining it is another. People might test your

limits, especially if they are used to you always saying "yes." Calmly and kindly repeat your boundary. Over time, they will understand you are serious.

Step 5: Show Empathy in Your Words and Tone
When you say "no," do it in a way that shows you understand their feelings. "I see how important this is to you, and I wish I could help more. But I can't right now." This way, they do not feel dismissed—they see that you still care.

---

5. Balancing Empathy for Others with Empathy for Yourself

Self-Empathy Is Essential
Before you can truly care for others, you must care for yourself. That means getting enough sleep, taking breaks, and giving yourself emotional space. If you are constantly drained, your ability to empathize will suffer.

Watch for Signs of Compassion Fatigue
Compassion fatigue happens when you give so much empathy that you begin to feel numb or cynical. Common among caregivers, healthcare workers, or anyone who deals with intense emotional situations daily, it can creep up on you. Pay attention to feelings of exhaustion, irritability, or a desire to avoid people's problems altogether.

Set Aside 'Me Time'
Schedule a walk, a relaxing bath, reading a book—whatever recharges you. This is not selfish. It is self-preservation, allowing you to come back refreshed and ready to connect.

---

6. Empathy and Boundary-Setting in Different Relationships

Romantic Partners

- **Mutual Respect**: Partners should respect each other's alone time, privacy, and emotional capacity.
- **Joint Decisions**: If one partner is more empathetic and tends to "absorb" the other's issues, it might be wise to discuss how to share emotional loads more evenly.

- **Open Communication**: Saying, "I need some time to decompress after work before I dive into a deep conversation" can be a healthy boundary.

Family

- **Parents and Adult Children**: Sometimes parents expect ongoing emotional or financial support. You can lovingly say, "I want to help when I can, but I can't solve everything. Let's find a different approach."
- **Siblings**: Rivalries or old patterns can lead to guilt trips. Being aware of these patterns helps you say, "I love you, but I can't talk about that subject anymore today."
- **Extended Family**: Family gatherings or cultural obligations can be stressful. You can set boundaries around how long you will stay or which topics are off-limits.

Friends

- **Time Commitments**: If a friend constantly invites you to events and you feel stretched thin, be honest about needing quiet nights at home sometimes.
- **Emotional Support**: If a friend leans on you heavily, suggest they also seek professional help or other friends, so you are not the only support.
- **Reciprocity**: Healthy friendships are a two-way street. If you are giving all the empathy but never receiving understanding in return, reevaluate how much you can continue giving.

Workplace

- **Saying 'No' to Extra Tasks**: If your plate is full, you can politely decline more responsibilities. "I'd love to help, but my schedule is booked. Could we discuss a future time or reassign some tasks?"
- **Professional Boundaries**: Keep personal sharing at a level you are comfortable with. If coworkers pry, you can say, "I prefer not to discuss that at work."
- **Empathetic Leadership**: If you are a leader, encourage a culture of respect for boundaries—like not expecting emails replied to at midnight or on weekends.

7. Handling Pushback or Guilt Trips

Sometimes, when you set boundaries, people may react poorly. They might accuse you of being selfish or say "You used to help me all the time—why change now?" It is important to stand firm yet remain empathetic:

Acknowledge Their Feelings
You can say, "I hear that you're upset because this is different from how I used to respond." This shows you understand their viewpoint.

Reaffirm Your Boundary
Then you gently repeat your limit: "I still want to support you, but I cannot do it in that way anymore." You do not need to over-explain or justify yourself with a long story. A concise statement can be enough.

Avoid Getting Defensive
If they try to guilt you, keep a calm tone. Remind yourself that setting boundaries is healthy. Over time, they may adjust to the new dynamic, or you might discover who respects your well-being and who does not.

---

8. When Empathy Alone Is Not Enough

Some situations demand more than empathetic listening and boundary-setting. For example:

Serious Mental Health Issues
If someone close to you is dealing with severe depression, anxiety, or suicidal thoughts, empathy matters a lot—but so does professional help. Encouraging them to see a therapist or call a helpline is crucial. You cannot be their only lifeline.

Abusive Relationships
If a person is abusive—whether physically, emotionally, or verbally—no amount of empathy on your part can fix the abuse. In such cases, boundaries may involve ending contact, seeking legal protection, or finding professional resources.

Toxic Work Environments
If your workplace disrespects boundaries, piles on unrealistic tasks, or fosters

bullying, empathy might help you cope, but you may need to talk to HR, find a new job, or pursue other formal steps.

In these cases, empathy is still important, but it must be paired with decisive actions to protect your safety and mental health.

9. Supporting Others in Their Boundary-Setting

Respect Their Limits
If a friend or family member tells you they have a new boundary—such as not wanting to discuss certain topics—respect it. Show empathy by saying, "I understand that this topic is sensitive for you. I'll do my best to avoid it."

Offer Encouragement
Some people feel guilty about setting boundaries. A supportive statement like, "It's good that you're looking out for yourself," can reassure them they are doing the right thing.

Avoid Taking It Personally
If their boundary reduces the time they spend with you, it may sting at first. Try to see that they might be overwhelmed or need to focus on personal matters. Empathy means understanding their perspective instead of immediately feeling offended.

10. Practical Exercises for Combining Empathy and Boundaries

1. Yes/No List
Write two columns: one for things you are okay saying "yes" to, another for what you need to say "no" to. Include tasks, topics, or emotional burdens. Seeing this on paper can clarify your boundaries.

2. Role-Play
With a friend or supportive person, practice boundary-setting conversations. For example, pretend your friend is a relative who wants too much of your time. This helps you refine how you say "no" or propose alternatives in a calm, empathetic manner.

3. Emotional Check-In

After a conversation where you set a boundary, reflect: "How did I feel? Did I remain calm? Was my tone respectful? Did I communicate the boundary clearly?" This self-awareness helps you improve next time.

4. Gratitude Balance

List things people do for you (like emotional support, kind words, or practical help) and what you do for them. A balanced list suggests healthy boundaries. If the list is very one-sided (you doing everything or them doing everything), consider adjustments.

---

11. Knowing When to Adjust Boundaries

Boundaries can change over time. For example, you might become more open or more strict depending on your life circumstances. It is okay to revise your boundaries as you grow:

- **Life Transitions**: A new job, a baby, or an illness might shift your energy and time, requiring fresh limits.
- **Recovery from Burnout**: After resting and healing, you might open up a bit more.
- **Increased Capacity**: As you become more self-aware and resilient, you might handle certain emotional demands better.

Stay flexible, but not so flexible that your core needs are not met. Regularly check in with yourself to see if your boundaries still serve your well-being.

---

12. Summary

Setting healthy boundaries does not mean tossing empathy aside. In fact, it can **strengthen** your empathy by ensuring you have the emotional resources to truly care for others without harming yourself. Boundaries protect your mental and physical space, let you recharge, and keep relationships fair and respectful.

- **Boundaries Are Protectors**: They help prevent burnout and resentment.

- **Empathy Still Flourishes**: You can say "no" with kindness and understanding.
- **Different Relationships, Different Boundaries**: Romantic partners, family, friends, and coworkers may require unique approaches.
- **Facing Pushback**: Some may resist your new boundaries, but maintaining them calmly reinforces your well-being and signals respect for yourself.
- **Evolving Limits**: Over time, boundaries can shift based on life changes and personal growth.

When empathy and boundaries work together, you can be there for others in a genuine, sustainable way. You do not have to sacrifice your mental health or personal comfort. In the next chapter, we will step back and look at how empathy shapes **our communities** as a whole. We will see how individuals with healthy empathy skills can influence neighborhoods, schools, and society at large, creating a more caring, supportive environment for everyone.

Chapter 15: How Empathy Shapes Our Communities

When people hear the word **"empathy,"** they often think of personal interactions—comforting a friend, talking with a loved one, or handling conflicts at work. However, empathy also has a much wider impact. A single act of kindness can spread through a neighborhood, a workplace, or even an entire city, changing the way people connect with each other on a daily basis. Communities are not just groups of people living in the same area; they are webs of relationships, ideas, and shared experiences.

In this chapter, we will look at how empathy can shape and strengthen the places we live—from small acts of neighborly care to organized efforts that promote social well-being. We will explore the role empathy plays in schools, local organizations, public services, and more. By the end, you will see that a community with empathy at its core can improve the quality of life for everyone, creating a sense of unity and warmth that lifts people up and offers support to those who need it most.

---

1. The Ripple Effect of Empathy in Communities

One Small Act, Many Outcomes
Empathy can have a "ripple effect." Imagine a person who helps an elderly neighbor carry groceries. That neighbor, feeling touched, might later decide to volunteer at a local food pantry to pass along the kindness. People who witness or hear about such acts might be inspired to do something similar. Soon, a chain reaction of supportive gestures can spread through a community, all sparked by one empathetic deed.

Building Trust and Safety
When neighbors or community members show empathy—by checking in on each other, offering help during difficult times, or just listening—trust grows. People feel they are surrounded by friends, not strangers. This sense of safety encourages them to participate in local events, support community initiatives, and speak up about common needs (like park improvements or safe streets).

Preventing Isolation
In many places, people do not know their neighbors or feel lonely despite living close by. Empathy cuts through that isolation. A friendly hello, a shared conversation about each other's lives, or a simple offer of help can remind someone they are not alone. Over time, communities with empathetic values tend to have lower rates of loneliness, depression, and social conflict.

---

2. Empathy in Neighborhoods and Local Groups

Informal Acts of Care
Empathy is often seen in small, everyday gestures. Neighbors might share tools (like a lawnmower or ladder) so that each person does not have to buy their own. Someone might leave fresh produce from their garden on another's doorstep. During a snowstorm, one family might shovel the walkway for the elderly couple next door. These acts cost little but build strong bonds of goodwill.

Neighborhood Watch or Community Alerts
When people genuinely look out for each other, a neighborhood becomes safer. Empathy fuels the desire to keep everyone protected. That might mean forming a neighborhood watch group or using a text thread or social media page to alert each other of concerns—like suspicious activity or missing pets. Rather than seeing security as an "every person for themselves" issue, empathy leads neighbors to see it as a shared responsibility.

Local Festivals and Gatherings
Public events—like farmers' markets, street fairs, or holiday parties—provide opportunities for community members to meet, share stories, and learn about each other's backgrounds. Empathy develops naturally when people spend time together, discover shared interests, and realize that even if their backgrounds differ, they have common hopes and challenges.

---

3. Empathy in Schools and Educational Programs

Teaching Children Empathy Early
Schools are a key place to foster empathy. Classroom activities that promote

group projects, peer mentoring, or conflict resolution show children how to cooperate and listen to each other. Teachers who model empathetic behavior—like using kind words, mediating fights calmly, or giving praise for helpful actions—help shape children's beliefs about how to treat others.

Anti-Bullying Campaigns
Many schools now have anti-bullying programs that emphasize empathy. Rather than just punishing bullies, these programs teach students to understand how bullying feels for the victim. By encouraging students to step in (safely) or report bullying when they see it, schools create a culture where children learn that caring for others is the norm.

Community Service Projects
Some schools require or encourage community service as part of the curriculum. Students might clean up a park, collect canned goods for a food bank, or visit a retirement home. These experiences let them see the impact of giving their time to help others. They see real faces and hear real stories, which can foster deeper empathy than reading about issues in a textbook.

---

4. Empathy in Public Services

Healthcare
Hospitals and clinics that focus on empathetic care often have better patient satisfaction. When nurses, doctors, or reception staff show understanding—taking a moment to reassure a scared patient or patiently explaining a confusing diagnosis—patients feel safer and more supported. This can improve their overall healing process and reduce stress for both patients and healthcare professionals.

Law Enforcement
In some areas, community-based policing practices teach officers to build relationships with residents, not just enforce rules. By hosting events like "coffee with a cop" or community forums, officers and citizens have a chance to talk, share concerns, and see each other as human beings, not just uniforms or potential suspects. Empathy in law enforcement can reduce tensions and help solve problems collaboratively.

Social Services

Empathy is crucial when helping vulnerable groups—like the homeless, refugees, or families in crisis. Caseworkers who listen with genuine care, who see clients as individuals with unique backgrounds, can make a huge difference in whether these individuals feel motivated to seek help or regain stability. Empathy also motivates the broader community to support or fund programs that assist those in need.

---

5. Empathy in Local Businesses and Economy

Customer Care

Local shops or restaurants that treat customers with empathy often flourish. Staff who remember regular customers' names or preferences build loyalty. When business owners care about the community, they might sponsor local sports teams or events, further blending commerce with care. This sense of belonging can also encourage residents to shop locally, keeping the economy vibrant.

Employee Well-Being

Businesses that foster empathy within the workplace create happier employees, which can improve service and productivity. Offering flexible hours for parents, providing mental health resources, or having an open-door policy for concerns are ways that empathy can show up in a company. In turn, employees who feel supported treat customers with warmth and respect.

Fair Practices

Empathy in the economic realm includes fair wages, ethical sourcing, and environmentally friendly policies. When business owners empathize with workers and the environment, they are less likely to exploit either. In such communities, people tend to have better working conditions, and local ecosystems face less harm.

6. Community Building Through Shared Projects

Cultural Exchanges
Events that celebrate different backgrounds—like potlucks where everyone brings a dish from their culture—help community members appreciate diversity. Empathy grows when people learn about each other's traditions, holiday customs, or family stories. It also counters prejudice by showing that behind every cultural label are real people with hopes, joys, and challenges.

Neighborhood Improvement Projects
Whether it is building a community garden, painting a shared mural, or fundraising for a new playground, joint projects unite people under a common goal. Working together, they see each other's talents, struggles, and dedication. This "we're in it together" mindset roots empathy in community bonds.

Volunteering and Mentorship
Mentorship programs that pair adults with youth can be powerful. An empathetic mentor provides guidance, listens to problems, and shares life lessons. Likewise, volunteering at shelters, food pantries, or literacy programs helps people meet neighbors they might not otherwise cross paths with, sparking a sense of connection and concern for others.

---

7. Challenges to Empathy in Communities

Busy Lifestyles
Modern life can be hectic. Long work hours, commutes, and packed schedules leave little time for getting to know neighbors. This lack of casual interaction can limit opportunities for empathy to develop. Breaking this barrier might require intentional planning—like community gatherings outside typical work hours or online forums where neighbors can chat.

Fear and Suspicion
In some places, crime or social tensions can make people wary of strangers. Empathy can seem risky if you are worried about safety. But complete isolation can worsen fear. Small gestures, like sharing information or having a neighborhood watch, can gradually rebuild trust.

Cultural and Language Differences
In diverse communities, people might feel unsure about interacting with those who speak a different language or follow different customs. Miscommunication can spark misunderstandings. Overcoming this requires patience, open-mindedness, and sometimes community-led language classes or interpreters who help bridge gaps.

Digital Disconnect
While social media can connect us to people far away, it can also disconnect us from the folks living right next door. Some communities find that neighbors do not meet in person because they spend their free time online. Creating local social media groups that encourage real-world meetups can help balance digital life with face-to-face empathy.

---

8. Practical Steps to Increase Community Empathy

1. Regular Community Gatherings
Scheduling monthly potlucks, game nights, or coffee mornings in a local park or community center can help neighbors build friendships. Even if only a few people attend at first, word may spread, and more will join.

2. Local Support Circles
A group for single parents, a book club, or a walking club for seniors—these smaller circles can form bonds where empathy thrives. Members share challenges and help each other out, feeling less alone.

3. Community Skill-Sharing
Workshops where people teach each other skills (like gardening, cooking, or computer basics) not only build practical knowledge but also foster respect and empathy. Teachers feel valued, and learners feel supported.

4. Open Communication
A community bulletin board (online or in a physical location like a library or cafe) where people can post announcements or needs (like "I need a ride to the grocery store" or "We're hosting a clothing swap") encourages a culture of mutual help.

5. Encourage Youth Involvement
Empowering teens to plan events or lead projects gives them ownership in the community. When young people feel heard and respected, they develop empathy for others and learn leadership skills that can shape the future.

---

9. Personal Reflection: Your Role in the Community

Start Where You Are
If you want to see more empathy in your neighborhood or city, begin with simple actions: greet neighbors, help someone carry groceries, show patience in crowded areas, or strike up a friendly chat at a local event. These small steps can start a chain reaction.

Volunteer
Look for local charities, soup kitchens, animal shelters, or youth programs that need help. Volunteering puts you in direct contact with people who have different life experiences, expanding your perspective and your empathy.

Join Local Groups or Boards
If you have time, consider joining a neighborhood council, a planning committee, or a school board. Your empathetic viewpoint can influence decision-making, ensuring that community policies consider people's well-being, not just numbers or convenience.

Share Positive Stories
When you see acts of empathy—like someone fixing up a neighbor's fence or organizing a fundraiser—talk about it. Share it on social media, mention it to friends. Positive stories motivate others to do the same and help shift the community's mindset toward compassion.

---

10. The Bigger Picture: Empathy and Social Change

Communities that embrace empathy often pave the way for broader social change. When enough people within a city or region treat each other kindly, larger projects can emerge—like creating community centers, improving public transportation for those who cannot drive, or developing affordable housing.

Government officials are more likely to respond to proposals if they see widespread community support rooted in compassion. In fact, empathetic communities can influence policy discussions around healthcare, education, and social welfare.

Collaboration with Authorities
When people approach city council meetings or town halls with respect and empathy—acknowledging the complexity of decisions—officials may be more willing to listen and collaborate. Instead of a shouting match, conversations become respectful dialogues where both sides try to understand each other's constraints and goals.

Leading by Example
Sometimes, an empathetic community becomes a model for other places. Maybe a city launches a successful program to support homeless individuals with not just shelter but job training and mental health services. That success story might inspire neighboring regions to adopt similar strategies. Little by little, empathy can spread far beyond one place.

---

11. Summary

Empathy is a powerful force that can transform communities from groups of people living near each other to supportive networks of neighbors and friends. We see it in small acts—like helping a neighbor rake leaves—or larger efforts—such as organizing inclusive events that bring people together. Schools that focus on empathy produce kinder students; businesses that value empathy treat workers and customers well; and public services that embrace empathy create safer, healthier environments for everyone.

- **Ripple Effect**: One act of kindness can spark many more.
- **Schools and Public Services**: Empathy in education, law enforcement, and healthcare builds trust and cooperation.
- **Local Businesses**: Caring about employees and customers promotes loyalty and fairness.
- **Practical Steps**: Community gatherings, volunteer opportunities, and open communication channels all spread empathy.

- **Social Change**: Empathetic communities can shape policies and inspire broader movements.

Next, we will shift our focus to **empathy's impact on leadership** in Chapter 16. We will see how empathy can guide leaders—from small local groups to large organizations—and how that leadership can ripple outward, affecting teams, organizations, and even entire industries.

Chapter 16: Empathy's Impact on Leadership

Leadership comes in many forms—managing a small team, running a large company, leading a volunteer project, or even guiding a nation. While traditional leadership often focused on authority, modern leadership is increasingly about collaboration, emotional intelligence, and empathy. Leaders who understand and care about their team's feelings tend to create more loyal, motivated, and creative teams.

In this chapter, we will explore why empathy is key to good leadership, how it drives better decision-making, how it influences workplace culture, and what pitfalls to avoid. Whether you are leading a startup, heading a department, or simply guiding a small group project, empathy can be the missing piece that turns an average leader into a truly inspiring one.

---

1. Why Empathy Matters in Leadership

1. Fostering Trust
Team members who feel their leader genuinely cares about them are more willing to share concerns, offer ideas, and be honest about mistakes. This trust allows leaders to spot issues early and celebrate good ideas that might otherwise stay hidden.

2. Reducing Turnover
In workplaces, high turnover (people quitting often) can be costly—both in time to find new hires and in lost expertise. Leaders who show empathy can detect signs of employee burnout, frustration, or personal struggles before they escalate. Employees who feel understood and valued tend to stay longer.

3. Boosting Morale and Engagement
When leaders recognize employees' efforts, listen to their suggestions, and celebrate small wins, morale goes up. People are more likely to go the extra mile because they see their work as meaningful and their leader as supportive.

4. Encouraging Innovation
Creativity thrives in an environment where people are not afraid to share unusual ideas. If a leader responds to new suggestions with curiosity rather than

dismissal, team members feel safe experimenting. Empathy helps leaders see the potential in these ideas and the passion behind them.

---

2. The Skills of an Empathetic Leader

Active Listening
We have discussed active listening in a previous chapter, but for leaders, it is even more vital. Instead of cutting someone off or jumping to a conclusion, an empathetic leader encourages the speaker to elaborate. They might ask clarifying questions or rephrase what they heard to ensure understanding.

Emotional Awareness
Leaders must be tuned in to both their own emotions and those of their team. That means noticing when tension is rising in the office or sensing when an employee is frustrated or sad. By recognizing these cues, they can address problems faster instead of letting them fester.

Open Communication
An empathetic leader sets the tone for transparent, respectful dialogue. They make it clear that questions, concerns, and even disagreements are welcome, as long as they are shared respectfully. This builds a culture where people do not hide problems.

Adaptability
Every team member is unique, with different goals, personalities, and stressors. Empathetic leaders adapt their style to meet each person's needs. For instance, some employees might appreciate direct feedback, while others might need a softer approach.

---

3. Empathy in Different Leadership Settings

1. Business and Corporate Leadership
In a corporate environment, empathetic leaders might hold one-on-one check-ins to ask about workload or personal well-being. They ensure employees have the resources they need, whether that is training, flexible hours for family, or mental health support. When layoffs or big changes happen, they

communicate openly, acknowledging the emotional impact and offering assistance where possible.

2. Community or Nonprofit Leadership
Leaders in charitable organizations often deal with people in crisis—like the homeless, disaster victims, or refugees. Empathy is central to their work. Nonprofit leaders must balance budget constraints with compassion for both clients and staff. They might meet volunteers personally, thank them for their effort, and ensure that no one feels overlooked.

3. Educational Leadership
School principals or university deans who practice empathy will regularly connect with teachers, students, and parents to see what challenges they face. They might set up "listening tours" or feedback sessions where people can voice concerns. This helps shape policies (like grading methods or mental health support) that truly serve the school community's needs.

4. Political Leadership
Politicians who value empathy might hold town halls, listen to constituents, and seek solutions that help the most vulnerable. They work with empathy-based policies—like healthcare, housing, or welfare programs—that acknowledge real human struggles. While politics can be divisive, leaders who maintain empathy can foster unity and collaborative solutions.

---

4. Linking Empathy with Strong Decision-Making

There is a myth that empathy makes leaders too "soft" to make tough calls. However, empathy and logic can coexist and even complement each other:

Gathering Better Information
When leaders listen empathetically, they get more honest feedback. Employees or citizens are more likely to share problems if they feel safe. This fuller picture helps leaders make decisions based on real facts, not just assumptions.

Weighing Impact
Empathy reminds leaders to consider how decisions affect people's lives. For instance, if a budget cut would mean layoffs, an empathetic leader might explore

alternatives or at least provide support like severance packages or job placement help.

Building Consensus
When people feel heard, they are more likely to support decisions—even if the outcome is not exactly what they wanted. An empathetic leader can say, "I understand your concerns. Here's why we are choosing this approach, and how we will try to lessen any negative effects." This approach fosters cooperation rather than rebellion.

---

5. Workplace Culture Under Empathetic Leadership

1. Psychological Safety
A key factor in high-performing teams is psychological safety—the knowledge that you can speak up without fear of punishment or humiliation. Empathetic leaders foster this by encouraging questions, feedback, and even constructive criticism. Employees learn that mistakes are opportunities to learn, not reasons for shame.

2. Inclusivity and Diversity
Empathy drives leaders to respect different backgrounds, voices, and experiences. They ensure hiring practices are fair and that people of varying ethnicities, genders, or abilities feel welcome. In an empathetic workplace, employees are judged on their work, not on stereotypes.

3. Healthy Conflict Resolution
Conflicts will arise whenever people work together. Empathy allows leaders to mediate calmly, acknowledging each side's emotions and guiding the team toward a fair solution. Rather than letting tensions simmer or taking sides, empathetic leaders promote understanding.

4. Growth and Development
Leaders who empathize see employees as whole people with ambitions, fears, and personal goals. They might offer coaching sessions, skill-building workshops, or simply recognition for good work. By encouraging people to grow, they nurture loyalty and a sense of purpose.

---

6. Pitfalls and Limits of Empathy in Leadership

Emotional Overload
Leaders who are highly empathetic can become overwhelmed by the emotional burdens of many people. They might feel they need to fix everyone's problems. To avoid burnout, leaders must set their own boundaries—knowing when to delegate issues or take a break.

Difficulty Making Hard Choices
Sometimes leaders must decide on layoffs, budget cuts, or ending certain projects. Empathy helps them handle these decisions humanely, but it does not eliminate the sadness or stress that comes from negatively impacting someone's life. Leaders should remember that caring about people does not mean never making tough calls; it means making them carefully and compassionately.

Bias Toward Certain Groups
Unconscious bias can color empathy. A leader might naturally empathize more with people who share their background or personality. Recognizing this bias is crucial. True empathy extends to everyone, not just those who are "like us."

Misreading or Over-Apologizing
In some cases, a leader might try so hard to be empathetic that they over-apologize or assume blame that is not theirs, creating confusion about accountability. A healthy balance involves listening, validating feelings, but not always taking on guilt for problems outside one's control.

---

7. Strengthening Empathy Skills as a Leader

Self-Awareness
We have discussed building self-awareness before. Leaders need to routinely check their own emotional state and be aware of triggers, stress levels, or personal biases. This introspection helps them stay balanced and present for their teams.

Seek Feedback
Ask your team members how they feel about the workplace environment. What could be improved? Where do they feel unheard? Listening to this feedback

without becoming defensive shows them you genuinely care. It also helps you see blind spots you might have missed.

Mentorship and Coaching
Learning from other empathetic leaders can be powerful. If you have a mentor who demonstrates compassionate leadership, observe how they communicate. Ask for advice on tough situations you face. Over time, you can develop your own empathetic style.

Take Courses or Workshops
Some leadership training programs specifically focus on emotional intelligence, conflict resolution, or communication. These can sharpen your listening skills and teach strategies for handling emotional conversations in a leadership role.

---

8. Real-World Examples of Empathetic Leadership Impact

Company Success Stories
Consider companies known for good employee relations—often, you will find empathetic leadership. For example, some tech firms encourage employees to set flexible schedules or work remotely when needed. They understand that people have families, commutes, or personal health issues. Such compassion often leads to committed, innovative workers who stay for the long term.

Public Figures and Movements
Leaders in social movements—like civil rights or environmental campaigns—often inspire people with empathy for those who are marginalized or for the planet itself. For instance, a leader might use personal stories of people hurt by pollution to make the issue feel real and urgent. This emotional appeal can move large crowds to action.

Local Heroes
Sometimes the most impactful leaders are not famous. They are community organizers, volunteers who coordinate disaster relief, or small-business owners who rally the town to raise funds for a family in need. Their empathy for people's struggles gives them moral authority and the respect of those around them.

9. Leading in Crisis Situations with Empathy

Urgent Decisions, Thoughtful Tone
During crises—like natural disasters or a pandemic—leaders must act quickly. Empathy guides them to communicate clearly, share updates without hiding bad news, and show compassion for those affected. While they cannot fix everything instantly, their empathetic demeanor fosters calm and cooperation.

Rebuilding Trust After Crisis
If a company faces a scandal or a city deals with a major accident, empathetic leadership is essential for rebuilding trust. A leader might apologize publicly, promise to investigate the root causes, and support those harmed. Words of empathy must be backed by concrete actions—like donating funds or changing policies—to show genuine care.

Encouraging Community Solidarity
In disasters, empathetic leaders encourage neighbors to help neighbors. They recognize that official resources might be limited, so they empower volunteers, share essential information, and ensure no one is left alone in their struggle. This approach can unify a community in the face of adversity.

---

10. Finding Balance: Results and Relationships

Some assume leaders must choose between getting results or caring about people. In truth, empathy can fuel better outcomes. A happy, valued team is more productive. Customers treated with genuine respect return for more business. Communities that trust their leaders are more likely to follow guidance or contribute new ideas. The key is balancing empathy with clear goals, accountability, and strategic thinking.

Measuring Empathy's Impact
Leaders can track turnover rates, employee satisfaction surveys, or community engagement to gauge if empathetic approaches are working. If employee happiness goes up and turnover goes down, it is a sign that empathy is making a difference. If public meetings are well-attended and feedback is constructive, you know your empathetic communication is reaching people.

Adapting Over Time

Leaders grow as they face new challenges. Early on, a leader might struggle to respond effectively to emotional conflicts, but with practice and learning, they can refine their empathetic approach. Each experience—whether a success or a stumble—adds to their emotional intelligence toolkit.

---

11. Summary

Empathy is not a weakness in leadership; it is a strength that fosters trust, innovation, and unity. By actively listening, showing genuine care for team members' well-being, and making decisions with people's feelings in mind, leaders can guide their organizations or communities to better outcomes. Empathy helps leaders:

- **Build Trust and Loyalty**: People stay when they feel respected and understood.
- **Encourage Growth and Creativity**: Safe, supportive environments allow new ideas to bloom.
- **Manage Conflict**: Respectful and empathetic mediation eases tensions.
- **Navigate Crisis**: Empathy in communication and action reassures and unites people in tough times.

Leading with empathy does not mean avoiding tough choices. Rather, it means handling them with compassion and fairness, explaining decisions clearly, and offering support where possible. This blend of empathy and accountability creates a leadership style that people can truly stand behind. In the chapters ahead, we will dive into **exercising empathy for personal growth** (Chapter 17) and explore **practical exercises** (Chapter 18) to keep sharpening this essential life skill.

Chapter 17: Exercising Empathy for Personal Growth

Most of this book has explored how empathy connects us to others—whether family, friends, coworkers, or entire communities. But empathy is not just an external skill. It also deeply affects our personal growth. By strengthening empathy within ourselves, we learn to navigate our own emotions better, open up to new experiences, and become more resilient in the face of challenges. Empathy influences how we see ourselves, how we understand our past, and how we build our future.

In this chapter, we will discuss how empathy—especially the kinds directed inward and outward—can lead to personal growth. We will cover how empathy helps us manage change, deal with setbacks, and discover new parts of ourselves. We will also see how empathy supports healthier habits, deeper relationships, and a more profound sense of meaning in life. By the end, you will have a clearer picture of how cultivating empathy isn't just about helping others—it's about helping yourself become a more balanced, grounded, and compassionate human being.

---

1. How Empathy Fuels Inner Change

Seeing Our Own Blind Spots
Empathy encourages us to consider others' viewpoints. But this effort often reflects back on us, too. The more we try to see the world through different eyes, the more we notice our own assumptions, biases, and habits. In short, empathy can serve as a mirror, revealing parts of ourselves we might otherwise ignore. A moment of compassion—like trying to understand why a coworker is upset—might lead us to realize we have been dismissive of others' stress for a while. This new awareness can spark a personal shift toward greater humility and attentiveness.

Gaining Self-Confidence
Self-confidence might seem unrelated to empathy, but when we connect deeply with others, we often discover that many of our private struggles—fears, self-doubts, or regrets—are not unique. Seeing that others share these feelings

makes us realize we are not alone. That sense of belonging can boost our confidence. We think, "If they can face their challenges, maybe I can, too." Empathy exposes our common humanity, calming the voice that says we are uniquely flawed or weak.

Overcoming Past Hurts
In previous chapters, we talked about emotional wounds and self-empathy. When we apply empathy to ourselves, we gently explore past hurts with kindness instead of shame or denial. Over time, this process can free us from old resentments or regrets. By treating our own memories and scars with the same gentle curiosity we would offer a friend, we learn to let go of blame, heal, and move forward with a cleaner emotional slate.

---

2. Building Stronger Resilience Through Empathy

Turning Anger into Understanding
Stressful events—like losing a job, having an argument with a partner, or failing an important test—can fill us with anger or hopelessness. Empathy, however, allows us to step back and see the wider story. Instead of lashing out, we might ask ourselves, "What other factors are at play?" or "If I were in my boss's shoes, how might I see this situation?" This shift from blame to curiosity reduces anger. It also opens a path to problem-solving. For example, if you get laid off, an empathetic approach might help you realize the company itself is struggling—not just targeting you personally—so you can plan your next move without the added weight of bitterness.

Facing Failures with Self-Kindness
Whether it's a missed goal at work or a broken relationship, failures can knock down our self-esteem. Self-empathy reminds us that mistakes are part of being human. Instead of harsh self-criticism, we can ask: "What can I learn here?" and "How can I treat myself kindly while I recover?" This positive mindset doesn't erase the pain, but it prevents it from paralyzing us. By being gentle with ourselves, we can bounce back more quickly and keep our sense of worth intact.

Coping with Uncertainty
Life is full of unknowns—health scares, financial worries, or simply not knowing where we will be in five years. Empathy, applied to ourselves and others, fosters

patience and calm in uncertain times. We see that everyone is navigating life's unpredictability. That realization can lessen our anxiety. It also reminds us that leaning on each other, sharing hopes and fears, is a normal response in times of confusion. This connectedness can make uncertainty less isolating and more manageable.

---

3. Empathy as a Path to Self-Discovery

Discovering New Interests

When we truly listen to people from different walks of life, we get glimpses into experiences, hobbies, or career paths we might have never considered. A friend's passion for painting might spark our own curiosity about art. A coworker's enthusiasm for volunteering at an animal shelter might lead us to try it, too. Empathy—genuinely caring about what interests others—can open doors to new experiences that broaden our horizons.

Expanding Emotional Range

Many of us find certain emotions uncomfortable—perhaps jealousy, grief, or vulnerability—and try to avoid them. However, empathy leads us to confront these feelings in a safer, more understanding way. For instance, if a friend shares a deep loss, being there for them might stir up our own feelings of grief. While this is hard, it also teaches us about our capacity to feel—and to survive—intense emotions. Over time, facing a wider range of feelings can make life richer and deepen our emotional maturity.

Refining Personal Values

Listening carefully to others can also challenge our personal values. We may meet someone whose beliefs differ from ours. Empathy asks us to see where they come from, which might lead us to reshape our own moral compass. For example, hearing a refugee's story might change how we view immigration policies or global conflicts. Empathy can refine or even shift our sense of right and wrong, moving us beyond inherited ideas to more thoughtful, compassionate stances.

---

4. Empathy's Role in Healthier Habits

Emotional Eating and Other Coping Mechanisms
Sometimes, when stress hits, we turn to quick fixes—junk food, too much alcohol, or excessive screen time. Empathy for ourselves might help us notice the root cause: "I'm not hungry, I'm just upset about the argument earlier." Recognizing this emotional need, we might choose a healthier coping strategy: talk with someone, take a walk, or practice deep breathing. In this way, empathy leads us to treat our bodies and minds with more care, reducing harmful habits.

Motivation for Exercise
Many people struggle with sticking to fitness routines. Empathy can help here, too. Instead of berating yourself for "laziness," you can say, "I understand why I feel tired—I've been stressed at work. But maybe a light walk would help me feel better." By acknowledging feelings and then offering gentle encouragement—like how you'd support a friend—you might be more motivated to move. The same logic applies to adopting better sleep habits, balanced diets, or mindful relaxation. Empathy replaces self-shaming with self-support.

Accountability in Social Circles
When friends or family share health goals with us—maybe quitting smoking or running a 5K—empathy helps us be supportive rather than judgmental. We encourage progress, listen to setbacks, and avoid pushing them too hard. As a result, we create a circle of mutual respect and accountability that helps everyone stay on track. This cooperative atmosphere benefits our personal growth as well because we see how mutual support drives real change.

---

5. Deepening Personal Relationships

Strengthening Friendships
Genuine empathy keeps friendships alive. When we truly hear our friends' worries, cheer on their dreams, and check in during tough times, those bonds grow stronger. We also learn about our own strengths—like how we can listen without judgment or offer practical help. Each time we show empathy, we refine our ability to connect.

Encouraging Honest Communication

Relationships thrive on open dialogue, but it can be scary to reveal our deepest thoughts or fears. Practicing empathy in personal relationships means creating a safe space for honest sharing. When we see our partner, sibling, or close friend speaking candidly, we may feel braver about voicing our own truths. In turn, each side's openness encourages the other, leading to a healthier and more intimate bond.

Resolving Long-Standing Conflicts

Some relationships—perhaps with a distant parent or an old friend—might have unresolved tensions. Empathy can open a door to reconciliation. By trying to understand their perspective, we can find a path beyond blame. This doesn't mean ignoring our own hurt. Rather, we acknowledge it while also allowing space for the other person's feelings. Over time, that empathy can thaw icy conflicts and even rebuild a relationship that seemed lost.

---

6. Finding Purpose and Meaning

Connecting Individual Purpose with Community

Earlier chapters described how empathy shapes communities. This link also works in reverse: by engaging empathetically in our neighborhoods or volunteering for causes we care about, we may discover a deeper sense of purpose. Helping a family in need or mentoring a teenager struggling with school can give us a clearer idea of what we value most in life. We realize that our personal growth is tied to the well-being of those around us.

Reflecting on Strengths

Empathy with others sometimes reveals gifts or talents we didn't fully appreciate in ourselves. Maybe people praise our ability to listen calmly, or our knack for organizing group events. Recognizing these strengths can guide us toward roles or projects that align with who we truly are. In turn, fulfilling those roles can add depth and joy to our daily lives.

Spiritual and Existential Reflections

For some, empathy can spark spiritual or existential questions: "Why are we here? How should we treat each other?" This might lead us to explore faith traditions, meditation, or philosophical readings that emphasize compassion.

Our personal growth might include discovering a spiritual path or forming a worldview centered on empathy and kindness.

---

7. Staying Balanced: When Empathy Overwhelms

The Risk of Emotional Drain
While empathy supports personal growth, too much empathy—especially if it leads to absorbing everyone else's pain—can overwhelm us. Empathy fatigue is a real issue, where we become emotionally worn out from constantly taking on others' troubles. This can lead to burnout or numbness, which then limits our ability to feel anything, for ourselves or others.

Knowing Your Limits
Personal growth includes recognizing that we have finite emotional bandwidth. It's okay to set boundaries (as explored in Chapter 14). For instance, if a friend regularly offloads intense problems on us at midnight, we can express care but also set a reasonable cutoff time for deep chats. By caring for ourselves, we keep our empathy sustainable.

Healthy Detachment
Sometimes, we must learn the difference between caring deeply and taking on someone else's responsibility. Being supportive doesn't mean we fix every problem for them. If a coworker refuses all solutions but keeps complaining, we may need to gently say, "I hear you, but I can't solve this for you." This helps maintain our own mental health and encourages them to take ownership of their issues.

---

8. Creating an Ongoing Practice of Empathy

Mindful Moments
Much like meditating or journaling, empathy can be woven into daily routines. For example, each morning, you might briefly reflect on someone in your life who could use a kind word. Or, when scrolling through social media, pause to really understand the feelings behind a friend's post rather than just skimming. Small mindful acts keep empathy active in your life.

Celebrating Progress
Growth is often slow and can feel invisible. If you notice moments when you responded more calmly, listened more patiently, or felt genuine compassion instead of judgment, give yourself credit. Recognize that these small steps build up over time, shaping a more empathetic you.

Self-Check Questions
Whenever you face a conflict or personal challenge, ask:

- "Am I showing understanding to the other person?"
- "Am I showing understanding to myself?"
- "What emotions are at play here?"
- "Is there a constructive way to handle these emotions?"

These questions can guide your actions toward empathy rather than letting stress or pride take over.

---

9. Examples of Empathy-Driven Personal Growth

Case: Overcoming Workplace Resentment
Consider someone who felt overlooked for promotions, building resentment towards their manager. By practicing empathy, they realized their manager was juggling many responsibilities and might not have fully seen their efforts. Instead of holding a grudge, they chose to communicate openly. This led to a better relationship and a chance to showcase their skills, ultimately furthering their career. In the process, they learned to address hurt feelings by seeking understanding, not by hiding anger.

Case: Family Healing
A young adult had a rocky relationship with a parent who was often absent during childhood. Growing empathy taught the adult to see the parent's own struggles—maybe they worked multiple jobs or lacked emotional support. While it did not excuse the hurt, it allowed for honest talks and a path toward forgiveness. The adult found personal peace, and the parent-child bond improved. In the end, empathy led to self-growth: less blame, more acceptance, and a healthier sense of identity.

10. Bringing Empathy into Future Goals

Personal Vision Statements
Some people write vision statements for their life—clear descriptions of who they want to be, what values they hold, and how they plan to achieve their goals. Incorporating empathy can be as simple as stating, "I aim to treat others with understanding and patience," or "I will value people's emotional well-being as much as outcomes." This clarity reminds us, amid daily chaos, that empathy is a key part of our long-term identity.

Career and Education Choices
We might also decide that we want a job or field of study that aligns with compassionate values—like social work, healthcare, education, or counseling. Even in corporate roles, we might choose a company known for ethical practices and supportive work culture. Alternatively, if we stay in a competitive industry, we might commit to being the empathetic voice within that space, influencing how things are done.

Legacy and Mentorship
As we grow older or take on mentoring roles, empathy becomes part of the legacy we pass on. We can teach younger people not just technical skills, but also the art of listening, caring, and collaboration. By modeling empathy, we help shape a future generation that values kindness as much as success.

---

11. Summary

Empathy is a powerful catalyst for personal growth. By seeing the world through others' eyes, we also learn more about our own fears, strengths, and aspirations. Empathy helps us handle setbacks with courage, uncover new passions, and connect with deeper purposes in life. It can inspire healthier habits, mend broken relationships, and guide us toward careers and life paths that reflect our true values.

- **Self-Discovery**: Empathy broadens our view, revealing blind spots and expanding our emotional range.
- **Resilience**: By treating ourselves with compassion, we recover from failures and manage stress more effectively.

- **Relationships**: Deeper empathy fosters honest communication, loyalty, and forgiveness.
- **Meaning**: Serving others or engaging empathetically in our communities can bring a sense of purpose and joy.

Of course, empathy requires balance. If we do not protect our emotional health, we risk burnout. But when done wisely, empathy for ourselves and others can be the key that unlocks new chapters of personal development—helping us grow, adapt, and find fulfillment in the journey of life. In the next chapter, we will move from discussing empathy as a mindset to showing you **practical exercises** that will strengthen your empathy skills. From short daily habits to deeper reflective methods, these tools can help you keep building empathy in a purposeful way.

Chapter 18: Practical Exercises to Strengthen Empathy

By now, we have explored empathy from many angles—its definition, its benefits, its challenges, and its role in personal and social change. But knowing about empathy is different from practicing it every day. Like any skill—playing the piano or cooking a new dish—empathy takes consistent effort. The good news is that there are many simple exercises that can help you become more empathetic.

In this chapter, we will dive into practical activities that strengthen empathy in daily life. Some are quick and can be done anytime; others involve more planning. You can try them on your own or with friends, family, or coworkers. The key is to approach these exercises with an open mind, patience, and the willingness to learn from missteps. Over time, these exercises can make empathy feel as natural as breathing, guiding how you talk, listen, and respond to the world around you.

---

1. Daily Micro-Practices

1. "30-Second Check-Ins"
Several times a day—maybe once every few hours—pause for 30 seconds. Notice who is around you or who might be on your mind. Ask yourself: "How might they be feeling right now?" Whether it's a coworker typing away at their computer or a parent who called you in the morning, put yourself in their shoes for a moment. Imagine what challenges or joys they could be experiencing. This habit keeps empathy front-and-center, even on busy days.

2. The "Look-Up" Rule
In public spaces, like a grocery store line or a bus, challenge yourself to look up from your phone. Observe the people around you. See if anyone seems anxious, tired, or happy. You don't have to stare or intrude—just note human expressions. This simple awareness fosters a mindset of caring and can gently remind you that everyone has their own story and feelings.

3. Gratitude for Helpers
When you see someone helping another person—like a store employee aiding a lost shopper—pause and mentally thank them. Recognize that an act of service, no matter how small, deserves acknowledgment. Practicing gratitude in this way encourages you to see kindness in everyday life, which can inspire you to do the same.

---

2. Reflective Listening Exercises

1. "Mirror and Clarify" with a Friend
Pick a willing friend or family member. Ask them to talk about something on their mind for a few minutes—perhaps a worry, a fun story, or a memory. While they speak, your job is to listen without interrupting. Once they finish, repeat back what you heard: "So you're feeling excited about your new job but also nervous about the commute, right?" Then ask if you got it correct. This exercise hones your active listening skills. It also trains you to clarify instead of assuming you know what they meant.

2. "No-Response Listening"
This variation is tougher. Have someone talk for two or three minutes about a personal topic while you remain quiet (except for natural nonverbal cues like nodding). After they finish, reflect in your own words what they shared: "I noticed you seemed really passionate when talking about your new art project." You can then discuss how it felt to speak freely without interruption and how it felt to only respond after. This can reveal how often we cut people off or quickly jump in with our own stories.

3. "Letter in a Bottle"
Ask a friend to write about a personal challenge or an emotional event (a few paragraphs). They give this "letter" to you. You read it quietly, reflecting on their perspective. Then, you write them a short letter back—only focusing on understanding their feelings and viewpoint, not giving advice or judging. This can be done with emails, too. It helps both parties practice empathy through written reflection.

3. Perspective-Taking Activities

1. Imagining Different Lives
Pick a random person you see during the day—a bus driver, a cafe server, or a stranger walking by. Quietly imagine a short story for them. Ask yourself: "Where might they have come from this morning? What might be on their mind? Are they excited about something or worried?" You are not spying or making big assumptions, just exercising your imagination to see different life contexts. This trains your empathy muscle to consider that everyone has a background we do not fully see.

2. Role-Switching with a Partner
With someone close to you, choose a scenario—like planning a vacation or solving a household problem. Then, "switch roles." If you are usually the one who picks the travel destination, let them lead this time, and you pretend you have their preferences. Listen as they outline what they want, and ask yourself how you would feel in their shoes. This activity teaches you to step out of your usual mindset and see the scenario from another angle.

3. Cultural Exploration
If you have access to cultural events, music, films, or foods different from your own upbringing, dive into them with genuine curiosity. Do not just taste a new dish—learn its story. Why is it important in that culture? This approach transforms a mere cultural experience into an exercise in empathy, helping you appreciate traditions and perspectives that differ from yours.

---

4. Emotion-Focused Methods

1. The "Emotion Wheel" Check-In
We discussed emotion wheels in earlier chapters. You can turn it into a regular exercise. Once a day, look at an emotion wheel (which lists core emotions like joy, anger, fear, sadness, and expands them into more nuanced feelings). Select which emotion(s) you are feeling at the moment. Then think of one person in your life who might also be experiencing a challenging emotion. Spend a minute imagining how that emotion impacts their day. This helps you tune into both yourself and another person's emotional life.

2. Empathy Journaling

Keep a small notebook or digital document where you note moments of empathy—both received and given. For example, if a coworker noticed you were stressed and offered help, write it down. If you found yourself caring deeply about a stranger's situation, note that too. Briefly describe how it felt. Over weeks or months, you will see patterns: what triggers your empathy, who you empathize with most easily, and where you might need more practice.

3. Music for Empathy

Music has a unique ability to stir our feelings. Pick a song that matches an emotion you or someone you know is experiencing—maybe heartbreak, hope, nostalgia. Listen to it closely, imagining the feelings in that person's mind. This helps you connect to emotions more directly. Some people even share playlists with friends as a way of saying, "I feel what you're going through." This merges art and empathy in a powerful way.

---

5. Group Empathy Exercises

1. "Highs and Lows" Circles

In a family, work team, or friend group, gather for a short session (maybe once a week). Each person shares one "high" (something good that happened) and one "low" (something challenging). No one interrupts. Listeners can ask clarifying questions after. This encourages empathy by letting people see each other's joys and struggles. It also normalizes open conversation, making future support more natural.

2. Collaborative Storytelling

Have a group create a short story together, each adding a sentence or two. The twist: before adding your part, you must reflect on how the current main character feels. For instance, if the character just lost their dog, you cannot jump straight to a happy ending without acknowledging sadness or searching. This exercise teaches a group to follow the emotional flow of a narrative, training them to notice feelings before making new suggestions.

3. "Walk in My Shoes" Workshop

This is more structured: each group member chooses a personal challenge they face—like stress balancing work and family, or anxiety about an upcoming event.

They present it briefly. Then the group, instead of giving advice, tries to restate how this challenge might feel. For example: "If I were you, I might feel overwhelmed and worried about letting people down." The person with the challenge simply listens and can clarify if needed. This builds a habit of responding with empathy rather than jumping straight to solutions.

---

6. Creative Expression for Empathy

1. Art Journaling
Instead of writing, grab colored pencils or markers and visually represent your day's emotions—or someone else's. You might draw swirling lines for confusion or bright shapes for excitement. This frees you from words, letting you access deeper feelings. If you do this while thinking of someone else's emotional state, you can reflect on what colors or shapes might fit their situation. This imaginative process develops emotional attunement.

2. Empathy Photography
If you enjoy taking pictures, use your camera to capture moments of connection or emotions. This could be a photo of a friend laughing, a stranger comforting a crying child, or an older couple holding hands. By focusing your lens on empathy in action, you train yourself to spot these gentle moments in daily life. You might even create a personal gallery or social media album titled "Everyday Empathy" to share positivity with others.

3. Story-Writing
Write a short fictional piece from the viewpoint of someone very different from yourself—a different age, culture, or life path. Research a bit if needed. Dive into their feelings, typical day, hopes, and worries. While it's fictional, this exercise challenges you to stretch your perspective. You might discover biases or new understandings along the way.

---

7. Virtual Empathy Tools

1. Online Role-Playing Games
Some interactive websites or games let you simulate experiences—like living on a

tight budget or navigating social issues. By playing these simulations, you gain a taste of what it's like in someone else's shoes. Reflect afterwards on how it affected your view of those realities.

2. Empathy Apps
A few apps guide you through daily empathy prompts, reflective questions, or mindfulness sessions aimed at building compassion. Look for apps that blend emotional check-ins with reminders to reach out to others. While technology can sometimes block empathy, the right tools can actually encourage it.

3. Global Friendships
If you have time and an interest in different cultures, consider joining a language exchange or international pen-pal platform. Consistent conversations with someone from another country can expand your empathy for global issues. Over time, you might exchange stories of daily life—learning how universal many experiences are, and also seeing unique cultural challenges.

---

8. Handling Common Roadblocks During Exercises

1. Feeling Silly or Awkward
Some of these activities might seem strange at first—like describing emotions, role-playing, or silently listening. Remind yourself that growth often happens outside your comfort zone. A bit of initial discomfort can lead to valuable insights.

2. Losing Focus
You might start a daily check-in exercise but forget to do it when life gets busy. Try setting phone reminders or tying the exercise to a routine (like during your morning coffee). Consistency is more important than trying to do it perfectly.

3. Emotional Overwhelm
If an exercise makes you relive painful memories or feel too emotionally raw, take a break. Consider talking to a counselor if deep issues surface. Empathy-building is meant to be constructive, not harmful. Listen to your emotional signals.

4. Facing Skepticism from Others
If you invite friends or coworkers to join an empathy exercise, some may mock it

or resist. Offer them an easy, low-stakes try, and respect their choice if they still decline. You can do many of these activities alone. Over time, they might grow curious, especially if they see positive changes in you.

9. Turning Exercises into Lasting Habits

Tracking Your Progress
Keep a small chart or journal where you note which exercises you practiced each day (or each week). Mark brief reflections like, "Today I did a 30-second check-in with my spouse in mind. I realized she might be worried about her meeting." Summarize how it felt. This simple tracking keeps you accountable and shows how empathy work accumulates.

Celebrating Milestones
If you manage to complete a certain number of empathy exercises—say 30 days in a row—treat yourself. It can be something fun: a favorite meal, a new book, or a relaxing activity. Tying small rewards to progress is not about bribery; it's about recognizing effort and maintaining motivation.

Adapting and Growing
Over time, you may find some exercises too easy or repetitive. That's a sign you are improving. Seek out new challenges—maybe deeper conversation formats or volunteering in emotionally demanding settings (like crisis hotlines or care centers). Each new step keeps empathy development alive and evolving.

10. Using Empathy Exercises in Different Settings

Personal and Family Life
These exercises work well with spouses, kids, and extended family. Doing "Highs and Lows" at the dinner table once a week, for example, can improve family closeness. Listening games can teach children how to be patient and considerate.

Work Environments
Empathy-building is crucial at work, too. Team-building events can include "mirror and clarify" or perspective-taking tasks. A "monthly empathy challenge"

in an office can encourage a friendlier culture. Just ensure these activities fit your workplace's tone—keep them professional but warm.

Community Groups
Clubs, volunteer organizations, or neighborhood councils can benefit from collaborative storytelling or "walk in my shoes" sessions. These shared experiences help members understand each other's backgrounds, leading to more effective cooperation on community projects.

---

11. Summary

Strengthening empathy is not just about big gestures or once-in-a-while moments of compassion. It thrives on consistent practice—small daily habits, deeper reflective methods, and creative group activities. The exercises in this chapter offer many ways to:

- **Tune into Other Perspectives**: Role-switching, mindful observation, and "mirror and clarify" all sharpen your awareness of others' feelings and thoughts.
- **Build Emotional Awareness**: Tools like an emotion wheel or empathy journaling help you see and express emotions clearly.
- **Encourage Thoughtful Communication**: Listening exercises teach how to give others space to talk, while perspective-taking activities broaden your approach to conflicts or decisions.
- **Foster a Culture of Care**: Group exercises bring empathy into families, workplaces, and communities, enhancing trust and cooperation.

Remember, empathy development is a journey, not a destination. It's fine to start small, pick one or two exercises that resonate with you, and then add more as you get comfortable. And if you skip a day or forget an exercise, don't fret—just pick it up again. Over time, these empathy habits can reshape how you view the world and how you engage with the people in it, making kindness and understanding a natural part of your everyday life.

Chapter 19: Teaching Empathy to Others

Empathy is a skill that can be learned, practiced, and improved. For many of us, it starts at home, in school, or within our social circles. Some people learn empathy more naturally—maybe they had caring parents or experienced kindness from a mentor. But not everyone grows up with the same examples. That is why **teaching empathy** can be such a powerful way to spread understanding and kindness through families, schools, workplaces, and communities.

In this chapter, we will explore how to teach empathy to people of all ages and backgrounds. We will look at methods for parents who want to raise caring children, teachers who hope to shape supportive classrooms, managers who aim to build a compassionate team, and everyday individuals who just want to help friends or neighbors become more aware of each other's feelings. By the end, you will understand that teaching empathy goes beyond lecturing; it involves modeling, guiding, and encouraging real-life experiences that make empathy come alive for others.

---

1. Why Teaching Empathy Matters

Breaking the Cycle of Conflict
When people do not learn empathy, they may grow up thinking only of their own needs. This can lead to bullying in school, toxic work environments, or aggressive driving on the roads. By teaching empathy early and often, we help reduce these harmful behaviors. People who learn to care about others' feelings tend to resolve conflicts with understanding, rather than force.

Promoting Respect for Differences
We live in a diverse world. Teaching empathy helps children and adults appreciate people who look different, speak another language, or hold different beliefs. They learn not to fear or mock these differences, but to try to see things from multiple viewpoints. This approach reduces prejudice and fosters more peaceful communities.

Raising Future Leaders
Tomorrow's leaders—whether they guide families, teams, or nations—will shape

our future. Leaders who have been taught empathy are more likely to listen, collaborate, and create inclusive policies. By instilling empathy skills now, we invest in a future where leadership values kindness and fairness.

---

2. Teaching Empathy to Children

1. Model Empathy in Everyday Life
Kids learn far more from what adults do than from what they say. If you show kindness—like comforting a distressed family member or treating a stranger politely—children notice. They see empathy in action. Parents and guardians can point out these moments: "Do you see how Aunt Sarah felt better after we listened to her? That's what empathy can do."

2. Encourage Emotional Vocabulary
Children are not born knowing words like "frustrated," "jealous," or "anxious." By naming these feelings when they arise, you give kids a way to describe their own emotions and recognize them in others. For instance, when a child loses a toy, you can say, "Are you feeling sad because you liked playing with that?" or when they see someone crying on TV, you might ask, "How do you think that person feels right now?"

3. Use Stories and Role-Play
Picture books, movies, or simple tales offer clear-cut scenarios. You can pause to ask, "How do you think the character felt when that happened?" or "If you were in their place, what would you do next?" These questions make children practice putting themselves in someone else's shoes. Role-playing works similarly: let them act out simple situations—like someone being left out at recess—and ask how they might show care.

4. Provide Real-Life Opportunities
Family chores and shared tasks can help children see teamwork and care. For example, if you have a family member who is sick, invite the child to help make them a get-well card or cup of tea. Or if there is a community drive, let them pick out cans for a food donation. Hands-on experiences teach that empathy is not just a concept; it is something we do.

5. Praise Empathetic Behavior
When a child shows a sign of empathy—perhaps comforting a sad sibling—offer

genuine praise: "That was so kind of you. I can see you really wanted them to feel better." Recognizing their efforts builds an internal motivation to keep caring about others. They learn empathy feels good and helps people around them.

---

3. Teaching Empathy in Schools

1. Classroom Culture of Respect
Teachers can set a tone where students feel safe to express themselves. Simple routines—like greeting each student warmly, encouraging questions, and celebrating different ideas—build a caring environment. This culture shows that everyone's feelings and opinions matter, which is the heart of empathy.

2. Group Projects and Collaboration
Assign group tasks that require listening and cooperation. For instance, if a science project demands each student contribute a part, they must value each other's input. The teacher can step in to highlight good cooperation, like saying, "Notice how Maya asked Carlos what he thought about the design. That's real teamwork."

3. Conflict Resolution Exercises
Inevitably, students will clash over small or big issues—maybe teasing or disagreeing on how to complete a project. Teachers can guide them to solve conflicts by calmly stating how they feel, listening to the other side, and seeking a fair solution. Over time, these guided conversations help students adopt an empathetic method of solving problems rather than accusing or ignoring.

4. Community Service and Field Trips
Service projects—such as visiting a senior center, cleaning up a park, or helping younger students—let children practice empathy. They see real needs in their community and realize they can help. Field trips to cultural centers or museums may also broaden their viewpoint, giving them glimpses into the lives and histories of different groups.

5. Reflection Activities
Teachers can end each week with a "circle time" or reflection session, asking: "Did anyone see an act of kindness or empathy this week?" or "What is something you did that helped someone else?" This ritual normalizes discussing empathy and helps students spot caring moments in everyday life.

4. Teaching Empathy in the Workplace

1. Lead by Example
If you are a manager or team lead, show empathy to your employees. This might mean checking in when someone seems stressed or acknowledging personal challenges like sickness in the family. An email saying, "I noticed you seemed overwhelmed today; let me know if you need any help" can build trust and model empathetic leadership.

2. Encourage Peer Support
Team-building events can include empathy-themed activities, like group discussions or exercises where each member shares a work challenge and others offer support (not just solutions). By making empathy part of team norms, you encourage coworkers to help each other out. This fosters a culture of mutual respect, rather than competition.

3. Offer Training Sessions
Some organizations hire experts to run workshops on emotional intelligence, active listening, or conflict resolution. These sessions can teach employees how to handle disagreements professionally and with empathy. Role-play scenarios—like dealing with a frustrated client—help employees practice responding calmly and kindly, even when under pressure.

4. Create Spaces for Honest Talks
Implement an "open-door policy" or schedule regular one-on-ones where staff can share concerns in a safe setting. This allows employees to speak up before problems grow. Hearing them out with empathy—acknowledging their viewpoint and feelings—improves morale. Even if you cannot fix every issue, showing you care helps people feel valued.

5. Celebrate Acts of Empathy
In company newsletters or team meetings, highlight moments when someone supported a colleague, handled a tough customer patiently, or helped a new hire feel welcome. Publicly appreciating these behaviors communicates that empathy is not just nice-to-have but a core part of your workplace values.

5. Teaching Empathy in Peer and Social Circles

1. Leading by Quiet Example
You do not need a formal role—like teacher or manager—to teach empathy. In your friend group, you can show empathy by listening attentively, asking thoughtful questions, and encouraging fair turn-taking in conversations. Others may notice your warmth and try it themselves. Over time, this can shift group norms.

2. Introducing Conversation Starters
At social gatherings, you could propose deeper questions than usual small talk—like "What's been inspiring you lately?" or "How have you been handling stress these days?" This gently nudges people to share feelings and can spark a more empathetic flow of discussion.

3. Steering Away from Gossip
Gossip can harm empathy by promoting judgment rather than understanding. When friends start gossiping, you might say, "I wonder what might be going on in her life that caused her to act that way," shifting the tone to curiosity instead of blame. Over time, this reframes how your circle talks about others, encouraging empathy rather than mockery.

4. Peer-Led Support Circles
If you have a close group or club, consider creating a simple support circle. Members take turns sharing a personal challenge, and others respond with empathy—mirroring feelings, offering gentle questions, and avoiding judgment. This fosters a culture of care where everyone practices giving and receiving understanding.

---

6. Overcoming Challenges When Teaching Empathy

1. Resistance or Cynicism
Some people might mock empathy training or think it is "soft." They might have grown up in tough environments where showing care was seen as weak. With them, it helps to show empathy's practical benefits—like reduced conflicts, stronger trust, or better outcomes. Often, demonstrating empathy in action is more persuasive than lecturing about it.

2. Lack of Time
In busy classrooms, workplaces, or families, it can be hard to squeeze in "extra" empathy lessons. But teaching empathy does not always need separate sessions. It can be woven into normal tasks—like praising a child's kind act or asking a coworker how they are feeling during a lunch break.

3. Cultural Differences
In some cultures, direct expressions of care might feel odd or intrusive. Adjust your approach to respect local norms. Maybe a warm smile, a small helpful gesture, or a quiet note of support is more welcome than a lengthy talk. Empathy can adapt to different cultural styles while still holding onto its core message.

4. Deep-Rooted Hurt
If someone has been deeply hurt by others, they might struggle to believe in empathy. They could be guarded or suspicious. Here, patience is key. Consistent acts of kindness—without pushing—may gradually open them up. Also, encourage them to seek professional help if trauma is blocking their ability to trust.

---

7. Creative Methods for Teaching Empathy

1. Storytelling Workshops
Gather a group and have each person share a short personal story—maybe about a challenge or a meaningful moment. Listeners then reflect on what emotions they heard. This trains everyone to pick up emotional cues and practice responding with understanding, rather than jumping to conclusions.

2. Theater or Improv Games
Acting exercises—like improvising a scene where participants must show understanding toward another character—can make empathy feel more natural. This method is especially helpful for people who learn by doing. They can physically step into another role and feel, at least briefly, what that character might feel.

3. Empathy Book Clubs
Reading a novel, biography, or memoir can spark deep discussions about the characters' feelings. By asking, "Why do you think they acted that way? What emotions might have driven their choices?" readers learn to interpret and

empathize with complex personalities. A monthly meeting to talk about these themes can turn reading into a shared empathy lesson.

---

8. Digital Avenues for Teaching Empathy

1. Online Courses and Webinars
Many platforms offer short online lessons on emotional intelligence or compassionate communication. If you lead a remote team or have distant family, consider signing up together. After each session, hold a group call to discuss key takeaways.

2. Collaborative Platforms
Apps or websites that let people share personal stories—like certain forum groups or community apps—can be harnessed to teach empathy. Participants read others' experiences and leave thoughtful comments. Encourage guidelines: "Focus on understanding, not judging" or "Ask clarifying questions, not criticisms."

3. Virtual Reality Simulations
Though still emerging, some VR programs let you briefly "experience" life from another viewpoint, such as living with a disability or facing a challenging social situation. Schools and training programs can use these to spark empathy in students or staff by immersing them in someone else's scenario.

---

9. Checking the Results: How to Know if Empathy Is Growing

1. Observation
Look for changes in how people talk to and about each other. Are they quicker to help? Do they speak less negatively behind someone's back? Does the general tone in the classroom, office, or home feel calmer and friendlier?

2. Feedback or Surveys
In structured environments—like schools or workplaces—you can gather feedback. For instance, ask students, "Do you feel more comfortable sharing your feelings?" or ask employees, "Do you see improvements in teamwork?" Their answers can reveal shifts in empathy levels.

3. Self-Reported Feelings
Encourage learners to reflect on their own emotional reactions. A person might say, "I used to get annoyed at small mistakes, but now I pause and think about the person's viewpoint." Such comments show a real internal change.

4. Less Conflict
If conflict does arise, watch how quickly people can solve it or how respectfully they approach it. A strong sign of rising empathy is when disagreements don't spiral into personal attacks but move toward constructive solutions.

---

10. Sustaining Empathy Lessons Over Time

1. Continuous Practice
Empathy is not a "one-off" lesson. It needs regular reinforcement. Teachers, parents, or leaders can keep empathy alive by including it in daily or weekly routines—like morning check-ins in a classroom, or monthly empathy workshops at work.

2. Peer Mentoring
Encourage those who have embraced empathy to mentor newer members of the group. In schools, older students can guide younger ones. In workplaces, experienced employees can model empathetic communication for new hires. Peer mentoring grows a culture where empathy is passed along naturally.

3. Adapt and Evolve
As people grow and groups change, adjust your methods. Maybe your class is ready for more advanced empathy tasks like in-depth role-plays, or your team is willing to form a workplace "kindness committee." Keep track of the group's progress and push the boundaries gently so that everyone keeps learning.

4. Celebrate Milestones
It is motivating to recognize how far a group has come. If a classroom or department has shown marked improvement—less bullying, better teamwork—celebrate that. A simple ceremony or meeting to acknowledge the positive shift can remind everyone that empathy is worth the effort.

11. Summary

Teaching empathy to others can transform hearts, minds, and relationships. It allows children to grow into kind adults, schools to become safe learning spaces, workplaces to support staff well-being, and social circles to foster deeper connections. The methods can be simple—like modeling empathy at home—or more structured, such as training programs or group projects.

- **Children Learn by Seeing and Doing**: Role-modeling and giving real-life empathy tasks help them absorb these lessons deeply.
- **Schools Thrive with Empathy**: Classrooms that honor every voice and guide students in conflict resolution raise empathetic citizens.
- **Workplaces Gain Loyalty**: Companies that value empathy see better cooperation and staff retention.
- **Peer Influence Is Powerful**: Even without formal authority, you can shape your social circle by being a living example of kindness.

Of course, teaching empathy comes with challenges—like skepticism or time limits. Yet the rewards are great: healthier relationships, fewer conflicts, and an atmosphere where people feel heard and valued. In the final chapter, we will look at how all these efforts can guide us toward **creating a more empathetic future**, on both personal and societal levels. By building on the lessons shared throughout this book, we can help shape a world where understanding and caring become the norm for generations to come.

Chapter 20: Creating a More Empathetic Future

We have reached the final chapter of this journey through empathy. We have examined what empathy is, how it grows, how it helps us heal, how it improves relationships, and how it can even transform communities and leadership styles. But the question remains: **What will our future look like if we embrace empathy as a guiding principle?** And, just as importantly, **how do we keep building empathy so that our children, their children, and the generations beyond continue to benefit from it?**

In this chapter, we will wrap up the ideas we have shared by looking at practical steps for building a more empathetic society. We will consider the roles of education, technology, policy, and grassroots movements. We will also invite you to see yourself as part of this bigger picture—someone who can push empathy forward in large and small ways. While change on a big scale can feel overwhelming, remember that empathy itself begins with one person caring about another. Multiply that by thousands or millions, and you begin to reshape the world.

---

1. The Vision of an Empathetic Society

Less Isolation, More Connection
In a deeply empathetic future, people do not feel alone in their struggles. Neighbors check in on each other. Workplaces see employees as whole people, not just workers. Schools ensure every child feels safe and included. Online spaces, instead of being filled with hate or shallow comments, become places where people offer support and constructive dialogue. This might sound ideal, but with concerted effort, it is within reach.

Collaboration Instead of Division
Societies often face big problems—like poverty, inequality, or climate change. Addressing these challenges requires collaboration across political, cultural, and economic lines. Empathy gives us a common ground. When we stop viewing opponents as enemies and see them as fellow humans with fears and hopes, we can find shared solutions. Empathy does not erase disagreements, but it changes the tone, making us more willing to listen and compromise.

Respect for Each Individual's Worth
An empathetic future does not just serve those who are powerful, wealthy, or popular. It values everyone, including the marginalized—like people who face discrimination, those with disabilities, or people experiencing homelessness. Society recognizes that each person has a story and deserves compassion. Laws and policies reflect a commitment to dignity for all, rather than just protecting the interests of a few.

---

2. Fostering Empathy Through Education

1. Curriculum Reform
Schools can be a driving force in teaching empathy at a large scale. Imagine a curriculum that includes emotional literacy, conflict resolution, and community projects as core subjects, not just extras. Students could regularly practice active listening, learn about global challenges through stories of real people, and engage in cross-cultural exchanges—maybe pen pals with students in other countries. All these experiences build empathy across diverse backgrounds.

2. Teacher Training
Educators themselves need empathy skills to handle the wide emotional needs of their classrooms. Providing teachers with training on recognizing emotional cues, managing conflicts kindly, and encouraging inclusive classrooms can help them model empathy daily. This training also supports teachers' own mental health, which can sometimes be overlooked.

3. Intergenerational Learning
Communities could create programs where older adults mentor younger people and vice versa. This sharing of life experiences fosters empathy between generations. Young people learn from older adults' wisdom, while seniors feel valued for their knowledge and connected to modern issues. Such connections can reduce age-related stereotypes and loneliness.

---

3. Government and Policy Influence

1. Legislating Compassion
While empathy is personal, governments can pass laws and policies that encourage caring behavior. For instance, worker-friendly laws (like paid family leave or flexible working hours) show empathy for people's personal lives. Policies supporting mental health services indicate a society's commitment to emotional well-being.

2. Community Dialogues
Local governments can organize forums where citizens discuss issues in a respectful setting, guided by trained facilitators. This ensures that even heated topics—such as zoning, environmental rules, or social welfare—are approached with listening and understanding. These discussions can prevent polarization and promote compromise.

3. Transparent Communication
Politicians who practice empathetic communication—like holding town halls or online Q&A sessions—let citizens feel heard. When citizens trust their leaders' intentions, they are more likely to engage with civic duties like voting, volunteering, or serving on community boards. Over time, empathy between leaders and constituents can build a healthier, more responsive democracy.

---

4. Technology as a Tool for Empathy

1. Positive Social Media Spaces
Social media often gets blamed for creating echo chambers or fueling negativity. But imagine online communities designed with empathy in mind—where moderators gently guide conversations, remove hateful content, and encourage supportive replies. Some platforms are already moving in this direction, hosting groups dedicated to mental health support or constructive debates. By promoting kind interactions, technology can break down isolation and widen our empathetic reach.

2. Online Education
Distance learning can expand empathy lessons across the world. Video courses, live workshops, or interactive apps can teach empathy skills to anyone with an

internet connection. People in remote areas or busy adults can learn at their own pace. This breaks the limits of physical classrooms, bringing empathetic education to diverse populations.

3. Virtual Reality and Immersive Experiences
As VR technology grows, we may see more immersive experiences that let users "walk" in someone else's environment—like living a day in a refugee camp, experiencing visual or hearing impairments, or dealing with day-to-day challenges related to a specific disease. These simulations can provide powerful empathy boosts, turning abstract issues into personal, felt experiences.

---

5. Grassroots and Community Movements

1. Volunteer Networks
Community groups that focus on local needs—such as soup kitchens, tutoring programs, or homeless outreach—offer direct channels for practicing empathy. People who volunteer not only provide help but also learn about real struggles in their town or city. This face-to-face awareness often leads volunteers to become empathy ambassadors in their wider circles.

2. Social Entrepreneurship
Some entrepreneurs launch businesses that aim for social impact—like fair-trade shops, eco-friendly goods, or platforms that connect donors to small community projects worldwide. By putting empathy at the heart of their business model, they shift the focus from pure profit to human well-being. As these ventures grow, they can inspire others to blend compassion with innovation.

3. Faith and Civic Groups
Religious organizations and civic clubs (like Rotary or Lions Clubs) often champion charity and service. If they integrate explicit empathy training—teaching members how to truly listen to those they serve—they move from a charity mindset ("giving from above") to a partnership mindset ("working alongside people in need"). This shift fosters respect and mutual empathy.

---

6. Personal Actions that Propel Society Forward

1. Being a Role Model
All societal changes start at the personal level. When you apply empathy in daily interactions—like actively listening to a friend in crisis, helping a neighbor with groceries, or even gently responding to negativity online—you show what empathy looks like in practice. Others see it and learn. Small choices can ripple outward more than you might expect.

2. Speaking Up
When you witness cruelty or mocking, choose to calmly stand up for empathy. For instance, if coworkers belittle someone, you could interject, "I wonder what might be going on for them right now. Maybe we should reach out instead." These small moments of courage can shift the tone of a conversation and remind people that empathy is an option.

3. Mentoring or Coaching
If you have experience in empathy-based communication, consider mentoring someone who struggles with it. That might be a teenager in your family, a younger colleague, or a friend who has a history of conflict. Guiding them—showing how to listen better, reflect on feelings, and approach tense situations calmly—can make a lasting impact on their life and how they treat others.

---

7. Barriers to an Empathetic Future

1. Fear and Insecurity
People often resist empathy when they are afraid—afraid of losing power, control, or simply not being heard themselves. Some fear that being empathetic means giving up their own opinions. But empathy does not require agreement; it just asks for respectful understanding. Overcoming fear might involve building trust step by step, showing that empathy does not erase anyone's voice.

2. Systemic Issues
Large-scale problems—like inequality, racism, or corruption—cannot be solved by empathy alone. However, empathy can drive the moral force behind changing unfair systems. We still need new policies, laws, and institutional reforms. Empathy can be the catalyst that pushes leaders and citizens to take those steps.

3. Growing Distrust in Institutions

If people see government, media, or big corporations as dishonest, they may lose faith and tune out. Rebuilding trust may require transparent leadership and accountability. Empathy helps leaders see the public's concerns and address them honestly, which can slowly repair bonds between institutions and the people they serve.

---

8. Sustaining Momentum: Next Steps

1. Broadening Access to Empathy Education

We can promote empathy workshops in prisons, retirement homes, sports teams—any place where people gather. Many folks who never had a caring mentor can discover empathy through a short program or supportive group. Reaching out to these overlooked communities helps empathy spread across all social layers.

2. Supporting Research

Academics and psychologists continue to study empathy's effects on health, crime rates, and social well-being. By funding and sharing these studies, we show skeptics that empathy is not just a soft ideal but a measurable factor that improves lives. Facts and data can convince policy-makers and business leaders to invest in empathy-building initiatives.

3. Connecting Across Borders

With global challenges—like pandemics or climate shifts—it becomes clear that compassion cannot stop at national lines. Encouraging cross-border friendships, supporting international aid, and learning about global cultures can help us see humanity as one big family. When empathy stretches worldwide, issues such as refugee crises or environmental disasters might be tackled with a sense of global responsibility, not just national self-interest.

---

9. Your Role in the Ongoing Story

This entire book has shown that empathy is not only beneficial, but also achievable with mindful practice. You do not have to be a celebrity or politician to make a difference. You can:

- **Integrate empathy in your daily life**: Listen carefully, handle conflict gently, and remember everyone is dealing with their own struggles.
- **Mentor others**: Teach empathy where you can—your children, friends, coworkers, or community group members. Simple guidance, like showing how to listen better, can be a powerful ripple.
- **Keep learning**: Empathy, like any skill, requires ongoing care. Stay open to new methods, cultures, and experiences that expand your empathy range.
- **Speak kindly but firmly**: When faced with hostility or ignorance, respond with calm compassion. Show that caring does not mean backing down but standing up for values with understanding.

Every act—no matter how small—reinforces a culture of caring. When enough people do this, the entire social landscape shifts.

---

10. Looking Ahead

Harnessing Empathy for Future Generations

Children born today will face new technologies, environmental shifts, and social structures we can barely imagine. What will guide them in these uncharted waters? Empathy is a strong compass that helps navigate change while preserving our shared humanity. If we teach them to value empathy, they will be equipped to handle tomorrow's challenges with creativity and compassion.

Innovating with Heart

Advances in science, robotics, and artificial intelligence can go in many directions. If empathy shapes our choices, we will develop technology that truly serves people—like AI that supports mental health, or smart cities that prioritize well-being over profits. Empathy ensures that progress does not leave behind our most vulnerable neighbors.

Global Unity

Empathy can chip away at the walls—both literal and figurative—that divide nations. While conflicts are complex and sometimes rooted in history, a consistent global push to understand each other's stories and pain can build bridges. Empathy-based diplomacy or cultural exchanges might reduce tensions, one conversation at a time.

11. A Final Reminder: Empathy Grows with Action

Throughout this book, we have repeatedly seen that empathy is about **doing**—listening, sharing, volunteering, setting boundaries, and caring for ourselves and others. Thinking about empathy is important, but real change happens when you turn those thoughts into lived experiences.

So, as you conclude this final chapter, consider one action you will take—maybe an exercise from Chapter 18, or a plan to help your community, or a shift in how you approach disagreements. Write it down, say it out loud, or tell a friend. Let it be your starting point for creating not only a more empathetic personal life, but also inspiring empathy in the wider world.

---

12. Summary

"Creating a More Empathetic Future" means weaving empathy into all levels of society—our schools, workplaces, governments, technologies, and communities. It requires:

- **Education Reforms**: Teaching empathy skills from childhood onward.
- **Supportive Policies**: Shaping laws and systems that value human dignity.
- **Cultural Shifts**: Encouraging compassion in media, social forums, and daily life.
- **Personal Dedication**: Each person committing to practice empathy and pass it on.

This future is neither guaranteed nor impossible. It depends on the choices we make today, the conversations we hold, and the examples we set. By combining steady personal practice with collective efforts, we can nurture a world where empathy is not just a rare gesture but an everyday norm—a foundation upon which we build stronger families, fairer societies, and a kinder global community.

Thank you for traveling through these chapters on empathy. Your journey does not end here. **Keep learning, keep practicing, and keep sharing empathy**—with the people you love, the strangers you meet, and the generations who will walk in your footsteps. With every caring choice you make, you help shape the future into a place where understanding and compassion truly guide how we live together.

www.ingramcontent.com/pod-product-compliance
Lightning Source LLC
LaVergne TN
LVHW012107070526
838202LV00056B/5657